JACOB'S LADDER

BRIAN KEANEY

Hodder Murray

A MEMBER OF THE HODDER HEADLINE GROUP

Hodder Headline's policy is to use papers that are natural, renewable and recyclable products and made from wood grown in sustainable forests. The logging and manufacturing processes are expected to conform to the environmental regulations of the country of origin.

Orders: please contact Bookpoint Ltd, 130 Milton Park, Abingdon, Oxon OX14 4SB. Telephone: (44) 01235 827720. Fax: (44) 01235 400454. Lines are open from 9.00am to 5.00pm, Monday to Saturday, with a 24-hour message answering service. Visit our website at www.hoddereducation.co.uk

Cover illustration and design © David Mackintosh 2005
This edition typeset in 12/15pt Univers 47 Condensed
by Servis Filmsetting Ltd, Manchester
Printed in Great Britain by CPI Cox & Wyman.

A catalogue record for this title is available from the British Library

ISBN-13: 978 0340 94088 4

CONTENTS

1. VIRGIL

Jacob's eyes twitched open and he became aware that he was lying on the ground with his face pressed against the earth. Rather stiffly he sat up and looked around. He was in the middle of an enormous field. There was cropped grass beneath him, dotted here and there with tiny white flowers which seemed almost to glow in the twilight. Ahead of him, in the distance, he could see a line of trees. Nothing was moving in any direction.

What was he doing here?

He tried to remember how he had got there and why he had been lying on the ground, fast asleep, but there seemed to be nothing in his mind, absolutely nothing, as if he had opened the cupboard of his memory and found it entirely empty.

Anxiously he looked all round, hoping he would see something that would remind him of what he had been doing before he had fallen asleep, but there was nothing to see, just grass on three sides, the line of trees ahead of him and, above, a huge expanse of sky the colour of bruised flesh. He didn't like the look of that sky. It seemed to be full of a dull menace.

Fear began stealing over him, like ice-cold water

1

seeping through his veins. He must be able to remember something, he told himself. He sat very still and concentrated. Think! How did you get here?

But it was no good.

He stood up, feeling the need to stem the rising tide of panic threatening to overwhelm him. He made his hands into fists and held them out in front of him, squeezing them hard, as if physical force would calm him. It'll be all right in a minute, he told himself. Just be patient. It'll come back to you. Let's see, what do you know?

His name was Jacob. OK. What next?

Nothing.

That was it. That was the only thing he could remember. His name was Jacob. He put his hands on his head and tugged at his hair. This wasn't possible. He had to be able to remember something. If he could just summon up the smallest scrap, he was certain that everything else would come tumbling back. If he could just make a start.

He looked down at his clothes. He was wearing blue trousers, a green T-shirt and white shoes. Both the trousers and the T-shirt had irregular brown patches on them. He felt certain they were his clothes but he did not remember them.

Then something did stir, very deep in his mind, so deep that it was like the faintest whisper in an enormous cavern. What was it? His will stretched out to grasp it, like a blind man reaching for a candle, and suddenly he had it. He knew what it was; but with a dreadful sense of disappointment, he realised it was no more than a feeling, not a concrete fact. It was simply a conviction that he had lost something.

Not just his memory. Something different. Before he had lost his memory, he felt certain that he had lost something else. But he had no idea what it was. He sighed. This was no good at all.

What was he going to do? He had to get some help, that was obvious. He needed to find someone who knew where he was, someone who could tell him what he ought to do next. Wait a minute! What about his. . . ? What were they called? The man and woman who looked after him? What did you call them? There was a word for it. He felt like stamping his foot in frustration.

He found this inability to even remember the word for the people who looked after him deeply distressing. He tried to picture them in his mind but he couldn't. Would he even recognise them if he saw them again? If he met them right now? This was terrible. How could he possibly have got into this condition?

Well, it was no good staying here in the field and waiting for it to get dark, or for a storm to come, which by the look of things might not be all that long. He had to do something. He needed to get out of here. But which way should he go? He turned slowly in a complete circle, feeling hopelessly indecisive, but as he came round to face the trees again, he thought he noticed something moving in the distance. He looked more carefully and now he was certain that a man was walking towards him. He felt an immense surge of relief. Someone was coming to help him. Immediately he set off to meet him.

The man had clearly seen Jacob and was walking rapidly, so it was not long before the two of them drew

3

near. Now Jacob could see him more clearly he noticed that the man was wearing some sort of uniform, a grey tunic and grey trousers, and he found this reassuring. This was obviously someone in authority. He would know what to do.

The stranger stopped when he was still some distance away. He was tall and thin with short dark hair and an unsmiling face. He gave a slight nod when Jacob reached him. 'I've come to collect you,' he said.

'Thank you,' Jacob replied and he meant it. He really did feel grateful that someone had come to collect him. The burden of understanding would now be taken away from him. The man in the grey uniform would be able to explain what was happening.

'Where am I?' Jacob asked.

'In the field,' the man told him.

'How did I get here?'

'Don't bother about that now. Just come with me.'

'But I can't remember anything,' Jacob explained.

'Don't worry,' the man assured him. 'It's perfectly normal.'

'What do you mean, normal?'

'No one ever remembers anything when they wake up in the field.'

'Why not?'

'That's just the way it is. There's no point in making a fuss. Just come with me.' With that, the man turned on his heel and began walking back in the direction he had come.

Jacob hesitated. He was beginning to have his doubts about this man. The answers he had given were not at all

4

satisfactory but Jacob couldn't just let him walk away, so he ran after him. 'Where are we going?' he asked.

'To the river,' the man replied.

'What river?'

'The river on the other side of those trees.'

'Why are we going there?'

'You'll see.'

'But can't you tell me now?'

The man shook his head. 'It isn't far,' he said. 'Just be patient.' He didn't look at Jacob when he spoke. Instead he kept his eyes firmly fixed on the line of trees ahead.

Jacob studied him more closely as they walked along, trying to decide what sort of a person he was. Was he good? Or bad? Was it wise to trust him? He simply didn't know. The man's face was lined and there was a sternness about his features, as if he was more used to giving orders than answering questions. But he seemed to know what he was doing. Besides, what else could Jacob do? If he didn't follow this man, he would be left on his own and he couldn't bear the thought of that.

As he was thinking this, Jacob noticed a badge or symbol on the man's tunic. It seemed to be a head with two faces, each pointing in a different direction. It didn't hold any meaning for him and he was tempted to ask what it stood for, but there were so many other questions filling his mind that he dismissed it.

They had reached the trees by now and, without checking his pace, the man stepped into the wood with Jacob close behind. The trees grew very tall and straight, with smooth, slender trunks like pillars. Far above Jacob's head the leafy canopy cut out what little light there was, so that it was almost as dark as night in here and noticeably colder.

'You haven't told me your name,' Jacob pointed out.

'Virgil,' the man replied. He spoke almost too quietly for Jacob to hear, as if it pained him to release this information.

'How did you know I was going to be in the field?'

'It's my job to know.'

'What is your job, exactly?'

'Right now it's collecting you.'

'Yes but when you're not doing that, what do you do then?'

'None of your business.'

He spoke curtly, as if Jacob's enquiry had offended him. But why? Surely Jacob was only asking a reasonable question? The trouble was, he couldn't be sure what was reasonable because he couldn't remember anything. 'Look, I'm sorry,' he said. 'I'm not trying to be nosy. I just don't understand. I'm trying to make sense out of things.'

'I've already told you. Just be patient,' Virgil replied.

But Jacob couldn't be patient. 'You said it was normal for me not to remember anything,' he went on.

'That's right.'

'So that must mean I'm not the only one you've found in the field.'

A faint smile flickered over Virgil's lips. Then it was gone again. 'That's true,' he agreed. 'You're not the first. Won't be the last, either, I shouldn't think.'

'So how do people get there in the first place?'

'I can't answer that.'

'Why not?'

'Because I can't. Now listen, any minute now we'll be out on the other side. The river's right in front as you come out through the trees, so mind yourself.'

Jacob soon saw that Virgil was right. It was already getting lighter and the trees were thinning out. A few minutes later they were in the open again and directly in front of them was a huge expanse of dark brown water.

Virgil turned left and continued walking along a narrow path between the trees and the river. There was only room for them to go in single file now so Jacob followed close behind. On his right, the shallow water was choked with reeds and grasses and it was hard to tell exactly where dry land ended and the river began. Stagnant pools had formed between the smooth black rocks that stuck out of the riverbed and the dense vegetation of the bank; an oily sheen glittered on their surface. But further out the water was flowing freely and moving with the force of a considerable current.

Virgil turned and looked over his shoulder at Jacob. 'Here we are,' he said.

Jacob saw that they had arrived at a stone platform projecting a little way out into the water. A wooden rowing boat was tied up at the end. Virgil led the way along the platform and got into the boat. He looked expectantly at Jacob. 'Come on,' he said. 'We've got to get across before nightfall.'

Jacob hesitated. He didn't feel entirely confident about stepping into the boat. 'Is it safe?' he asked.

'Of course it's safe,' Virgil told him. 'Do you think I'd get in if it wasn't?'

Cautiously, Jacob stepped into the boat and sat down. Virgil untied the mooring rope. Then, picking up the oars, he pushed the boat away from the platform and began to row. The oars dipped into the water and were lifted clear again with mechanical regularity. Further out the water was no longer brown but almost black, reflecting the purple sky above.

Jacob found himself thinking once again about the man and woman who looked after him, whatever they were called. They would be wondering where he was right now, he felt sure of that. They would be worried about him. This thought was so strong, it was almost like a physical pain.

'There are some people who need to know I'm here,' he said. Again he struggled for the word. Suddenly it came to him. 'Parents,' he said. 'That's the word I was trying to think of. My parents. Someone should tell them. They'll be worrying.'

'Everyone knows who needs to know,' Virgil assured him.

'Are you certain about that?'

'I wouldn't say so if I wasn't.'

'But you've only just found me,' Jacob said. 'I don't see how they could have been told where I was.'

'Look, I knew where you were, didn't I?'

'Yes.'

'Well then. It's all in hand. All you have to do is stop fretting and let me get on with rowing this boat.'

It was clear that he was not going to provide any more

information so Jacob had to content himself with watching the trees behind them recede and the opposite bank gradually come closer. After a while he could make out buildings on the other side and his spirits began to rise. 'Do I live over there?' he asked.

Virgil nodded. 'Why do you think I'm taking you there?' he asked.

What a relief! Virgil was bringing him back to where he lived. Soon he would see his parents and perhaps there would be other people who knew him. They would probably be delighted to see him. They would explain everything. They would help him remember what had happened. For the first time since waking in the field, Jacob began to relax. His ordeal would soon be over.

He sat back in the boat and allowed one hand to trail in the water. But immediately he took it out again. The water was numbingly cold. He shook his fingers and put them under his armpit to warm them. Virgil saw what he was doing and gave another of his grim smiles. 'Colder than you expected?' he asked.

2. LOCUS

It was almost dark when they finally reached the other side of the river, tied the boat beside a set of stone steps and climbed up onto the quayside. To Jacob's disappointment there was no one waiting to meet them, just a huddle of low stone buildings grouped around a cobbled square with a dim lantern swinging creakily on a pole in the middle.

Virgil led the way across the square and up a narrow street that climbed steeply away from the river. The buildings on either side were of the same sort as those clustered around the harbour, squarely built of crude stone blocks and without decoration of any sort. 'What's the name of this place?' Jacob asked.

'Locus,' Virgil told him.

'Locus,' Jacob repeated. He had hoped the name would seem familiar but it caused not even a ripple of memory. Disappointed, he hurried along beside Virgil.

After about five minutes Virgil turned down a narrow lane and stopped in front of a building much like all the others. The same symbol Jacob had noticed on Virgil's tunic was carved above the door. Once again he wondered what it meant.

'Here we are,' Virgil announced.

Jacob held his breath. Would his parents be waiting for him? Virgil opened the door and they stepped inside.

The interior of the building was one long room with beds placed at regular intervals on either side. Boys of about Jacob's own age were sitting or lying on the beds and he noticed that they were all wearing grey uniforms like Virgil's. They fell silent as the newcomers stepped into the room and turned to look in their direction.

Virgil took no notice of them. 'This way,' he told Jacob and led him between the rows of beds until they came to one that was unoccupied. 'This is yours,' he said. Then, without waiting for a reply, he turned and walked out of the room.

Jacob wanted to call out after him, 'Wait! You haven't explained anything.' But it was too late. The door had closed and he was left standing by the bed. He could feel the eyes of all the other boys on him and he was not sure whether they were pleased to see him. He felt waves of disappointment wash over him. He had stood outside with Virgil, convinced that his parents would be behind the door. Instead he had walked into a room full of strangers.

'What's your name?' the red-haired boy on the next bed asked. He sounded friendly enough.

'Jacob.'

'Mine's Toby. Did you wake up in the field?'

'Yes.'

'I thought you must have done. Do you remember anything before you woke up?'

It seemed to Jacob that Toby was looking very intensely at him as he asked this. He shook his head. 'No.'

A collective sigh of disappointment went through the room.

A thought occurred to Jacob. 'Did you wake up in the field, too?' he asked.

Toby nodded. 'Everyone here did.'

'What is this place?' Jacob asked.

'It's called Locus.'

'Yes, I know that. But I mean, why are we here, do you know that?'

'We're here because we've got to be somewhere,' another voice said. Jacob looked in the direction of the speaker and saw a tall, well-built boy with thick, dark hair. He was sprawling on his bed on the other side of the room and he had a look on his face that suggested he thought Jacob's questions were tiresome.

'But what about . . .' Again, infuriatingly, Jacob found himself struggling for the right word. 'What about the place we were before we woke up in the field? Where our parents are. I can't remember the word for it.'

'Home,' Toby said.

Another collective sigh seemed to run through the room at the mention of the word.

'Yes,' Jacob said. 'That's right, home. I thought that was where Virgil was bringing me.'

'Everybody always thinks that,' the tall boy said. 'We have the same discussion every time anyone new arrives.'

'He doesn't know that, does he?' Toby said. 'He's just got here. Don't be so mean.'

The tall boy opened his mouth to reply but he was interrupted by a sound that rang through the building, resonating in the air around them and drowning out everything else. Immediately everyone began to get up and file out of the door.

'What is it?' Jacob asked.

'It's the bell for supper,' Toby told him. 'Come on, I'll show you where to go.'

Toby led the way out of the building and Jacob saw that the street outside, which had been empty when he first arrived, was swarming with boys and girls, all heading in the same direction.

'Don't take any notice of Stefan,' Toby said as they joined the throng.

'Who's he?'

'The tall boy with the dark hair who said we always say the same thing every time someone new arrives. He doesn't really mean to be unfriendly. He's just a bit odd.'

'In what way?'

'All sorts of ways. He won't join in with the memory game, for example.'

'The memory game. What's that?'

'Oh it's just something we do to pass the time. You'll see later. Look, here we are. This is the dining hall.'

They had been making their way through a series of narrow lanes and now Jacob saw that they had arrived in another cobbled square. In the centre stood an enormous stone building surrounded by crowds of boys and girls who were queuing up to pass through entrances on all four sides.

Toby led him towards one of these and they joined the queue.

'How long have you been here?' Jacob asked as they shuffled slowly forward.

Toby frowned. 'I'm not sure,' he replied. 'You lose track of time after a while. I was the last one to join our dormitory – before you that is. So I know what it feels like when you're standing in the middle of the room and they're all looking at you. But don't worry, they're all right really.'

His reply filled Jacob with dismay. The fact that he did not seem to know how long he'd been there suggested that it could have been a very long time indeed – days and days. More than days. But Jacob couldn't think of the word for longer periods of time. Even more depressing than the fact that Toby might have been there for a long time was the casual way he spoke about it, as if he had got used to the idea of living there. Well Jacob wasn't going to do that. He was going to get out of there and go back home, where he belonged. He wondered why everybody else didn't feel the same.

He looked round at the queues snaking out from all four sides of the building and wondered how many people there were here. 'How many dormitories are there?' he asked.

'I'm not sure,' Toby said. 'Lots. This isn't the only dining hall either.'

By now they had reached the double doors through which their queue entered the dining room. Jacob noticed the familiar two-faced symbol carved above the doorway. 'What does that mean?' he demanded.

'I don't know that either,' Toby replied. 'But it's everywhere.'

'Haven't you asked anyone?'

Toby shook his head. 'When you first arrive, you're full of

questions,' he said, 'but then, after a while, you just get used to things and you stop wondering about them.'

They were through the doors now and Jacob could see hundreds of boys and girls sitting at tables that were arranged in rows. Almost all of them were wearing identical grey uniforms except for here and there where an individual, like himself, was wearing distinctive clothes. At one of the tables a girl dressed in a red sweater stood out like a beacon. As Jacob looked more closely he saw that there were the same irregular brown markings on her clothes as he had noticed on his own. At that moment she looked up from her food and saw him staring at her. For a few seconds their eyes met, and Jacob thought he saw on her face the same helpless bewilderment he felt himself.

Toby noticed the direction of his gaze. 'Another newcomer,' he said.

By now they had reached the head of the queue. At a hatch behind a counter three uniformed women were handing out plates of some whitish substance Jacob did not recognise. They all looked so similar – pale-faced with short dark hair and thin lips – that they could have been sisters. He thought about asking them some of the questions filling his head but there were dozens of people in the queue behind him waiting their turn and, besides, he found the blank expression on the women's faces discouraging. He tried to catch the eye of the one who handed him his plate but her gaze seemed to slide over him, as if she did not really see him at all. He took his portion of food, picked up a knife and fork and followed Toby over to one of the tables. 'What is it?' he asked.

He poked it with a knife and it rebounded slightly, like a sponge.

'I don't really know,' Toby said. 'It's just what we get here.'

'What, every day?'

'Yes.'

'Don't you get fed up with it?'

Toby shrugged. 'It's not that bad really,' he said. He cut off a piece and put it in his mouth.

Gingerly, Jacob followed suit. He found it chewy and salty, neither pleasant nor unpleasant. But even though he was hungry, eating it felt like a chore.

A few tables away he saw the girl in the red sweater carrying her plate away to put in a stack of used crockery against the wall. He wondered what she had thought of the meal. But perhaps it had not been strange to her. Perhaps this was simply a common food that he couldn't remember. Somehow he doubted this, though. He had the feeling that this white spongy stuff was unique to Locus. It fitted in with everything else here.

He turned back to Toby. 'Why don't you leave?' he asked. 'I mean there's no lock on the door of the dormitory, is there? And there isn't someone watching you all the time. You could just walk out of here.'

'How can you leave if you don't know where you want to go to?' Toby replied.

'But you know you want to go home,' Jacob argued, 'and that's a start.'

As he was saying this, Stefan sat down beside them. 'Still talking about home?' he asked.

'Of course I am,' Jacob said. 'That's where I should be now, not here.'

'How do you know home is such a marvellous place?' Stefan asked. 'Can you actually remember anything about it?'

'I know how I feel when I think about it,' Jacob replied defiantly.

'It's not the same thing,' Stefan pointed out. 'I know how I feel about food when I'm hungry but then, when someone hands me a plate of this stuff, I feel differently.'

'That's because this isn't proper food,' Jacob objected.

'Are you sure about that?'

'I'm not sure about anything.'

'Exactly,' Stefan said. He looked pleased with himself.

'Why are you so keen to stand up for this place?' Jacob asked.

'I'm not standing up for it. I'm just being realistic. This is where you are and you might as well accept it. You're never going home, Jacob. No one ever goes home from here.'

He spoke with a chilling certainty but Jacob wasn't prepared to give up his hopes. 'Do you know where Virgil went?' he asked Toby.

Toby shook his head. 'No one can ever find him unless he wants to be found. Usually it's just to bring another new arrival.'

'Who's in charge here, then?' Jacob asked.

Toby shrugged. 'No one,' he said.

'There must be someone.'

'Well I don't know who it is.'

'What about the women serving food? They must know who's in charge.'

'There's no point in asking them anything,' Stefan said.

'Why not?'

'They don't speak.'

Jacob turned to Toby. 'Is that true?'

Toby nodded. 'No one's ever heard them say a word.'

'Well I'm going to wait here until they've finished serving,' Jacob declared. 'Then I'm going to see for myself.'

'You're in for a long wait then,' Stefan said getting up and taking his empty plate with him. 'See you back in the dormitory.'

'Why does he have to sound so pleased with himself all the time?' Jacob asked, after Stefan had gone.

'It's just his way of dealing with things,' Toby replied. 'I guess it's what works for him.'

'Yeah well it gets on my nerves,' Jacob said. He glanced over at the queue for the hatch where he had collected his food. It still stretched the whole length of the dining hall and out through the double doors. Stefan was right about one thing: he was in for a long wait. 'You don't have to stay here with me,' Jacob said. 'I don't mind waiting on my own.'

'That's OK,' Toby told him. 'It's not as if I've got anything else to do. Besides, you'd never find your way back to the dormitory by yourself.'

That was true. Jacob hadn't thought of that. The prospect of being lost all over again made him shudder. 'Thanks,' he said.

It took a long time for the queue to shorten but at last, when there were only a few more children waiting to be served, he got up and joined it. Toby came with him.

'Haven't you ever tried to speak to these women?' Jacob asked as they shuffled patiently forward.

'No.'

'Why not?'

'Stefan tried the day I arrived here.'

'Stefan?'

'Yes. I was sitting in the dining hall and I saw him go up to them and say something but they didn't reply so he started shouting at them.'

'What happened?'

'Nothing. They didn't take any notice.'

'I thought Stefan liked it here.'

'I wouldn't go that far,' Toby said. 'I think he's just got used to it, like the rest of us.'

By now there were only a couple of people in front of Jacob. He waited for them to be handed their food. Then it was his turn. The nearest of the three women held out a plate. Jacob shook his head. 'I've already eaten,' he said. 'I just want to know who's in charge.'

The woman didn't react at all. She simply continued to hold out the plate with the white, spongy cube of nameless food on it.

'I don't want any food,' Jacob told her. 'I want to speak to Virgil.'

Still her face remained impassive.

Jacob tried the woman next to her. 'Please,' he said, 'I want to speak to Virgil, or if he isn't here, then someone else in authority.'

But instead of replying, the second woman merely held out another plate of food.

'Look, I don't want any food!' Jacob told her. 'I want to speak to someone.'

Like her colleague, she gave not the slightest sign that she had understood him.

Frustration surged through Jacob. He took the plate and threw it onto the floor where it smashed into pieces. There was complete silence in the dining hall and all eyes turned in his direction.

Toby put his hand on Jacob's shoulder. 'Let's go back to the dormitory,' he said.

A moment later a door slid down, sealing off the hatch and the women who stood behind it.

Back in the dormitory the boys were sitting or lying on their beds just as they had been when Jacob first arrived. Stefan glanced in Jacob's direction as he and Toby made their way between the rows of beds. Jacob waited for him to make some sarcastic comment. He was ready to tell Stefan exactly what he thought of him. But Stefan only raised his eyebrows in a gesture that could have meant anything.

When Jacob reached his bed, he found a little pile of clothes there: pyjamas, underwear and a grey uniform. There was also soap, a towel and other toiletries.

'Who put this stuff here?' he demanded, looking round at the rest of the room.

One or two people shrugged. 'Someone brought it when we went to the dining hall,' Stefan told him. 'That's what it's like here. Everything happens when you're not looking.'

'I'm not wearing this,' Jacob said, holding up the uniform.

No one made any comment.

Not long after supper, the lights in the dormitory suddenly grew dimmer. This seemed to be the signal to get ready for bed. The boys got up and went through a door at the end of the dormitory which led to a bathroom. Despite the fact that he had been asleep only a few hours ago, Jacob found that he felt utterly exhausted. So although he followed the others into the bathroom, he was too tired to bother with a shower. Instead he washed his face, went back into the dormitory, put on his pyjamas and climbed into bed. A little while later the lights went out completely.

Jacob was drifting off to sleep when he was awakened by Toby's voice from the next bed. 'Who's going to start?' he asked.

Start what? Jacob wondered, but almost at once another voice from the opposite side of the dormitory began. 'I remember playing with a ball.'

As soon as he heard these words an image came into Jacob's mind. In it he was looking down at his feet and there, on the ground in front of him, was a ball. It was black and white and he was about to kick it. The image was so vivid it took his breath away.

'I don't know where I was,' the boy continued, 'but there was grass and mud and there were other boys there too. They were shouting at me but they weren't angry. It was a game.' He paused. 'That's all,' he concluded.

A moment later another voice began. 'I remember standing by a fire.' Once again a picture formed in Jacob's mind. He could see the yellow flames flickering back and forth, tongues of fire. 'There was smoke,' the speaker continued, 'and I remember that I liked the way it smelt.'

'I remember a dog,' a third voice said. 'It was my dog, I think, and I was stroking it. I was pleased with it because it had just done something. I don't remember what. But the dog was pleased too.' In Jacob's imagination a big brown dog was looking up at him, panting eagerly, its mouth stretched into a wide grin of pleasure.

After that there was silence for a while. Then Toby spoke again. 'Does anyone else remember anything?'

'Why don't you all go to sleep?' Stefan's voice said.

'Do you remember anything, Jacob?' Toby asked, ignoring Stefan.

Jacob desperately wanted to say yes. He would have loved to come up with a picture like the others had done. But there was nothing in his head except an aching to be home. Then he recalled the feeling he had experienced in the field. 'I can't really remember anything,' he said, 'except, I've just got this feeling that I've lost something. Not just my memory. Something else, but I don't know what it was.'

'Everyone feels that,' Toby told him.

'Oh.' Jacob felt disappointed. He had hoped it might mean something important but it seemed that it was nothing special after all.

'Never mind,' Toby told him. 'Things do come back after a while. Not everything, of course. Just little details every now and again.'

'To everyone?' Jacob asked.

'To everyone,' Toby assured him.

Jacob sighed and closed his eyes. It wasn't much but at least it was something to look forward to.

3. THE STONE FIELDS

The sound of the bell woke him the next morning. He sat up in bed, utterly bewildered at first, but then the events of the previous day came back to him. He could remember everything since he had woken up in the field. But before that there was still the same yawning chasm.

He reached for his clothes, which he had left at the bottom of the bed, but there was no sign of them. 'Who's taken my clothes?' he demanded, looking angrily around the dormitory.

'It'll be the minions,' Toby told him.

'Who are they?'

'They're like the women who serve the food. They keep the place tidy but no one ever sees them.'

'That's so annoying!' Jacob said. 'I want my own clothes back. I don't want to have to wear this uniform.'

But there was no alternative. The uniform fitted him perfectly but that was no consolation.

'You stop noticing it after a while,' Toby told him.

'I won't.'

Breakfast was exactly the same as supper, except that it included a mug of some hot drink which was brown in colour and somehow seemed to taste brown as well. While he ate, Jacob looked idly round the room for the girl in the red sweater but there was no sign of her. He wondered whether she, too, had woken up to find her own clothes had been taken away in the night.

'So what happens now?' Jacob asked when they had finished their meal.

'We go stone-picking,' Toby told him.

'What does that mean?'

'A bus comes and takes us outside the town to the stone-picking fields and then we have to fill up baskets with stones.'

Jacob could not make much sense out of this answer. He wasn't sure what a bus was — something to do with travelling, he was certain of that. And a basket — was that for carrying things? He decided that Toby was telling him they would be taken somewhere and made to work and he didn't like the sound of it.

'First we need to collect our packed lunches,' Toby went on. He led the way over to where hundreds of small boxes were set out on tables to one side of the dining hall. He handed one to Jacob. It was grey in colour, like almost everything else in this place and made of a material that was both strong and flexible. Jacob opened the top, which was hinged, to reveal a small glass bottle of a greenish-looking liquid and something wrapped in paper. It turned out to be more of the white spongy stuff they had just been eating.

'Is this all we get?' Jacob asked.

'I'm afraid so,' Toby told him. 'Come on, the bus will be waiting for us.'

As they walked back to the dormitory, Jacob thought

about the stone-picking that Toby had described. It sounded like hard work. 'What if you don't want to go?' he asked.

'That's not a good idea.'

'Why not?'

'Because of the ghosts.'

'Ghosts?' The word meant something frightening, Jacob was certain of that.

'This place is full of them,' Toby told him. 'You'll find that out if you stay behind.'

Jacob wanted to ask more, but they were back in the dormitory by now and outside, waiting on the street, was the bus. He recognised it immediately. It was big, blue-grey in colour with rows of seats for passengers, and already most of the boys from the dormitory were on board.

'I've been on one of these before,' Jacob said, excited at the way words were coming back to him in a flurry.

'Well we might as well get in,' Toby suggested.

Jacob hesitated. He wasn't sure whether this was a good idea or not. But all the other boys were going and then there was what Toby had said about the ghosts, whatever they were. Besides, there would surely be someone in charge in the stone-picking fields, someone who organised the work. That decided him. He got on the bus with Toby.

The driver was a young woman, less grim-faced than the ones who had served the food. She looked at Jacob as he clambered on board and gave him a brisk smile. 'Just arrived?' she asked.

Well at least she could speak. Encouraged, he sat down near her. 'I got here last night,' he told her.

'You'll soon get used to things.'

'I don't want to get used to things,' he replied. 'I want to go home.'

'Where's that then?' she asked him.

'I don't know.'

'Not much chance of getting there then,' she observed.

'I need to find someone who's in charge,' Jacob said. 'Who tells you where to drive every morning?'

'I've been coming here as long as I can remember,' she replied.

'But someone must have told you to come here in the first place.'

'Well of course they did.'

'And who was that?'

'Virgil.'

'That's who I want to see,' Jacob insisted. 'Can you tell me how I can find him?'

She shook her head. 'You don't find Virgil,' she said. 'He finds you.' She turned towards the back of the bus. 'Everyone on board?' she called out.

'We're all here,' someone shouted back.

She started up the engine and the bus pulled away.

They drove through the narrow streets of the town, between endless, identical grey stone buildings, travelling away from the river which Jacob and Virgil had crossed the day before. On the way they were joined by several other buses until there was a convoy steadily making its way out of the town.

At last they reached the outskirts of Locus and the buildings began to give way to open land. There was little vegetation here, just a few stunted trees and bushes clinging tenuously to the barren, stony ground. But after a while Jacob noticed a line of wooden huts on either side of the road. Areas of ground beside these huts had been roped off into squares and boys and girls were working within the roped-off areas, though he couldn't see exactly what they were doing. But they had not gone much further before the bus came to a halt beside one of these huts. The driver turned off the engine. 'Here we are,' she called out. 'Everybody off the bus.'

Inside the hut an old man with white hair was waiting for them. Beside him was a stack of what Jacob now recognised as baskets. Each of the boys handed over his lunch box, took one of the baskets and made his way over to the roped-off area nearby.

'Is Virgil around here?' Jacob asked.

The man turned piercing blue eyes on Jacob, studying him for a long time before shaking his head.

'I want to know when I can go home,' Jacob continued.

'I don't know anything about that,' the man told him. 'I'm just here to see that the stones get picked up.' He handed a basket to Jacob.

Despondently, Jacob followed the others. The ground here was covered with small stones and his job seemed to be to fill the basket with stones, carry it to the edge of the roped-off area for emptying and then begin all over again. The other boys seemed already to have settled into the rhythm of work.

Jacob went over to Toby. 'What's the point of this?' he asked.

'We're clearing this area so that they can build some more dormitories,' Toby told him. 'At least that's what Berith says.'

'Who's Berith?'

'The old man.'

Jacob bent down, picked up a few stones and put them in his basket. 'This is boring,' he said.

'You get used to it,' Toby assured him.

'That's what you say about everything.'

'Do I?'

'Yes you do. Anyway I'm not doing it. I don't see why I should.'

'You have to,' Toby told him.

'No, I don't.' He put the basket down and sat on the ground.

The next thing he knew, he was picking up a stone and dropping it in the basket. Startled to find himself doing this, he straightened up. A moment ago he had been sitting on the ground, determined not to do any work. Yet here he was picking up stones like everyone else. How had that happened? He didn't remember getting up and beginning again. Somehow or other he must have lost his concentration. Confused, he put the basket down again, sat on the ground and folded his arms.

He looked over in the direction of the hut and noticed, with a start, that Berith was staring straight at him. Even at some distance Jacob felt uncomfortable under his gaze. He turned round to face the other way. He needed to make a plan, he told himself. It was no good just asking to speak to someone in charge. They obviously weren't going to let him do that. So what was he going to do about it? He bent down, picked up another stone and put it in the basket.

What was he doing?

He straightened up. How had that happened? He had absolutely no memory of standing up, picking up the basket and resuming work but here he was, filling his basket like all the others, and, judging by the fact that there were quite a few stones in the bottom, he must have been doing it for some time.

He began to suspect that what Toby had told him was literally true. He had no choice but to pick up stones because every time he stopped, something or someone overrode his decision. He looked in Berith's direction. The old man had stopped staring at him. Nevertheless, Jacob couldn't help suspecting that Berith had something to do with this; there was something about his eyes that suggested he knew what you were thinking. Jacob turned his back on him.

He decided to concentrate on trying to get his memory back. If only he could remember what he had been doing before he fell asleep in the field. If he could just recall that, then surely he could work backwards from there. How had he come to be in the field in the first place? That was the question. He reached down, picked up another stone and dropped it into the basket.

He was doing it again!

Furious with himself, he turned the basket upside down and emptied the stones onto the ground. Then he turned round and stared defiantly in Berith's direction. But the old man had gone inside the hut. Jacob looked around for Toby and saw that he was at the edge of the roped-off area, emptying out his basket. He went over to him.

'I keep trying to stop,' Jacob told him. 'And then, before I know where I am, I'm picking up stones again.'

Toby nodded sympathetically. 'It's better just to get on with it,' he said. 'It only makes you more tired otherwise. You'll find that out after a while.'

He was right, of course. Before long Jacob had made up his mind that it was pointless to resist. However many times he decided he was not going to work, within a short space of time he found himself picking up stones again and putting them in the basket.

'If you don't try and fight it, it's easier to think,' Toby told him, as they worked side by side.

'What do you think about?' Jacob asked.

'I mostly try to remember things,' Toby replied.

'Do you succeed?'

'Sometimes. When I don't try too hard. You have to sort of let your mind float, if you know what I mean.'

Jacob nodded. He thought he knew what Toby meant but it wasn't easy because the same thoughts kept running through his mind over and over again. What had he been doing in the field? What had happened to his memory? And how was he going to get home?

In the middle of the day Berith came over to them, carrying the lunch boxes.

Everyone immediately put down his basket, took his lunch and sat on the ground. Jacob felt certain that Berith looked at him more intensely than at everyone else as he handed over his lunch box but he made no comment.

'I don't like that old man,' Jacob said. 'He gives me the creeps.'

'He's all right,' Toby said. 'You . . .

'. . . get used to him.' Jacob finished the sentence for him. 'I know. I'll tell you what though, I don't think I'm ever going to get used to this food.' He unwrapped his portion of the white spongy stuff and began to eat. 'Did you remember anything while you were working this morning?' he asked.

Toby shook his head. 'I couldn't seem to get into the right frame of mind,' he said. 'You have to let go of all your other thoughts but this morning I couldn't seem to do that.'

Jacob opened the bottle of greenish liquid and took a drink. It tasted sharp and quite refreshing but left a bitter aftertaste. 'I'm not coming here tomorrow,' he announced.

Toby looked doubtful. 'You'll regret it,' he said.

'No I won't,' Jacob told him. 'Those ghosts that you talked about can't be any worse than doing this all day.'

'Can't they? Why do you think we all come out here every day?' Toby replied.

'Because you've learned to accept it, that's why,' Jacob said, scornfully. 'That's not going to happen to me. I want to get out of here and go home and I'm not going to forget that.'

After a while Berith reappeared and told them that lunchtime was over. They handed over their empty lunch boxes and set to work again picking up stones.

Jacob found it easier in the afternoon. Perhaps it was because he had stopped resisting, as Toby had suggested. After a while he found that, like the others, he settled into

31

a rhythm, stooping to pick up a stone, straightening up to drop it in the basket, stooping down again. In time the regularity of his movements began to lull the incessant questioning filling his mind and he became less obsessed with thinking of how he could escape. It was then that he found himself remembering something. A picture came into his mind. In the picture he was kneeling down, bending over something, some sort of package, and he was tearing at the paper wrapped round it. He was feeling excited by the package because he was certain it would contain something really good. Suddenly he knew what he was doing: opening a present, a birthday present. Immediately the image was gone, like a bubble bursting. But it was enough. He stood up and ran over to Toby. 'I remembered something,' he said, excitedly. 'I remembered something.'

'Don't tell me,' Toby told him. 'Save it for tonight after lights out. Then we can all hear it.'

Jacob nodded. The idea pleased him. Tonight he would have something to contribute to the memory game. And for now he could savour every detail of his recollection. For the rest of the afternoon he smiled to himself as he worked.

4. GHOSTS

Jacob made up his mind over breakfast that he would not go to the stone-picking fields again. If the others wanted to wear themselves out, then that was up to them. But, as far as he could tell, there wasn't one good reason why he should join them. He certainly wasn't going to learn anything from Berith. The old man gave him the creeps. He'd be far better off staying in the dormitory until the bus had gone, then scouting around to see what he could learn about the way things were organised here. Maybe he would even be able to find Virgil.

He told Toby about his decision.

Toby had been munching steadily through his breakfast. Now his jaw stopped moving and his face took on a worried expression. 'I really wouldn't do that if I were you,' he said.

'But you're not me, are you?' Jacob said. He was tempted to add that he was a very different kind of person from Toby, that he was not the sort who just accepted a situation without challenging it. But he said nothing of this. He liked Toby and he had no wish to be unpleasant to him. All the same, in his opinion Toby, and the others too, were all too ready to give up at the first sign of difficulty. To get free from this place would require determination and although Jacob couldn't remember very much about himself, he knew one thing: he was the determined type.

Toby continued to look at him anxiously. 'What about the ghosts?' he asked.

'What are ghosts, exactly?' Jacob replied. 'I mean I know they're something frightening, but I can't remember much else about them.'

'They're dead people who come back to life,' Toby told him.

Jacob didn't like the sound of this. He could feel all sorts of unpleasant memories shifting under the surface of his mind. Dead people who come back to life – what would they be like? Would they want you to join them among the ranks of the dead? Would they try to kill you? Were there worse things than death? 'Has anybody seen them?' he asked.

'Some people have seen them, others have just heard them,' Toby informed him.

'But they weren't harmed?'

Toby shook his head.

'So what's all the fuss about?'

'I don't know,' Toby said. 'I've never tried to find out. I just know that once they've encountered the ghosts, nobody ever wants to repeat the experience.'

'Yes, well I don't want to repeat the stone-picking experience either,' Jacob said. 'I felt stiff when I woke up this morning. Every muscle in my body was aching. And don't tell me I'll get used to it because I don't intend to.'

'OK,' Toby replied. He shrugged. 'It's your decision. What

did you think of the memory game last night?' he added, changing the subject.

'It was good,' Jacob told him. Actually, 'good' was rather an inadequate word to describe the images and feelings that the memory game had conjured up in his mind. Already, he realised, he was looking forward to playing it again that night.

It was Toby who had begun, just as on the previous night, but this time Jacob had had a memory to share with the others and he wasted no time in telling them about it. As he had described it, the image had grown stronger in his mind so that it was almost as if he was living the reality of his memory all over again. For a moment he could see the room in which it had happened, feel the eyes of his parents watching him and sense the pleasure of their expectation. On the carpet in front of him was a little pile of presents of different shapes and sizes, each one wrapped in different paper. He reached forward and picked up the top present, tearing carelessly at the wrapping. He felt certain it would contain just what he wanted and he was filled with a happiness so complete and so natural, he didn't even think about it, didn't count himself lucky, didn't clutch at the pleasure and exclaim aloud. He was just a boy on his birthday and everything was going as he expected. He had a right to be happy. That was how he felt.

Then the image was gone.

'I wish I could remember more,' he said. 'It's so frustrating.'

'It's always like that,' Toby replied. 'You only ever remember fragments, but in a way that makes them more precious, if you see what I mean. Anyway, it's time we were getting back to the dormitory.'

'You go back,' Jacob told him. 'I'll hang on here for a bit. Tell the others I'm not coming, will you? And when the driver asks if everyone's on board, say yes. You can always say you thought I'd got on before you, if anyone asks afterwards.'

'Are you sure you're not going to change your mind?'

'I'm certain.'

'OK.' Toby got up. 'Good luck,' he said.

Jacob watched him go. Then he waited while the crowd in the dining hall thinned out. He thought about the decision he had made and took comfort from Toby's assurance that nobody had actually been harmed by the ghosts. What concerned him more was the possibility that, despite his resolve, he might find himself going back to the dormitory and climbing on the bus, just as he had found himself picking up stones against his will the day before.

He felt extremely conspicuous, sitting at the table by himself in the busy dining hall with an empty plate in front of him. Nevertheless, he made himself wait until there were only a few people left. Then he got up and slowly made his way out of the building.

He needn't have feared. There was no sign of the bus when he got back and the dormitory was empty. Feeling pleased with himself, he lay down on his bed. In a little while, he decided, he would go out and have a look around, but first he would lie low for a while, until there was no chance of someone discovering him and putting him on another bus.

What he needed to do, he decided, was to make a plan because the more he thought about it, the more certain he was that nobody here was going to help him. So if he was ever going to get out of here, he would need to rely on his own abilities.

It was while he was thinking this that he first became aware of the sound. It was so low that he wasn't sure at first he hadn't just imagined it. He sat up in bed, listening carefully. No, there it was again. This time he was certain. It sounded like someone whispering. Jacob looked all round the dormitory, though he knew perfectly well there was no one else there. Then he got up and went to look in the bathroom. He walked systematically past the doors of each cubicle, peering inside. The place was completely empty and there was nowhere that anyone could be hiding. He must have just imagined it, he told himself. Toby's story about the dead who came back to life had put him on edge, that was all. He went back to the dormitory, lay down on his bed and tried to concentrate on his plan of escape.

But no sooner had he done so, than he heard the noise again. This time it was louder and it was definitely someone whispering.

He sat up in alarm. 'Who's there?' he called out.

'Jacob,' said a woman's voice. It was as clear now as if the speaker was facing him. She pronounced his name in a way that sounded almost like an accusation, as if he had disappointed her in some way, or as if she held him responsible for some wrongdoing. And for some reason that he couldn't understand, Jacob felt an answering sense of guilt stirring inside himself.

'Who are you?' he demanded.

'Jacob,' the woman's voice repeated.

'I'm here!' Jacob said. 'What do you want?'

But instead of replying the invisible speaker began quietly to sob.

Jacob found this even more disturbing than hearing her call his name. 'What's the matter?' he called out.

The sobbing only grew louder.

'Please don't do that,' Jacob said. The weeping seemed to touch something deep inside him, a raw nerve he had been unaware he possessed. He felt as if some hidden, intensely sensitive part of himself was being twisted and torn by the woman's sobs. 'Please stop crying!' he begged.

But the woman took no notice. Her sobs grew louder still and more unrestrained until the outpouring of grief seemed to fill the whole dormitory.

'Stop it!' Jacob shouted. He put his hands to his ears but it made no difference. He could hear the weeping as clearly as if it were inside his own head.

He had to get out of the dormitory. He could not put up with this for a moment longer. He ran out of the room and immediately the sobbing stopped. He heaved an enormous sigh of relief. It was over. In a minute he would think about what it meant but first he just allowed himself to relax and let the horror slip away.

This must have been one of the ghosts that Toby had talked about. Well he was right when he said it was a dreadful experience. It was not one that Jacob would ever want to repeat. But it seemed that as long as he stayed outside the dormitory, he was safe. That was something to be grateful for. He wandered a little way down the road and sat on a low stone wall, trying to recover his composure.

He looked up at the sky. It was the colour of washed slate. The pale disc of the sun was just visible behind the blue-grey clouds, but it spread no warmth over the ground. Jacob shivered slightly. In a minute he would get up and go for a long walk, he decided. First, though, he needed to pull himself together.

Whose voice had it been? That was the question that filled his mind. He was sure that at some level of his being he recognised it. And the speaker had certainly recognised him, or at least she had spoken his name, though she had taken no notice of his attempts to talk to her. Indeed she had behaved almost as if she could not hear him.

As he was thinking this, something made him start. He sat up straight and looked around him. Had he imagined it or was it the same whisper that he had heard in the dormitory? He listened carefully.

'Jacob.'

Oh no! It couldn't be starting again. Not out in the open. He got to his feet, a terrible sense of panic beginning to take hold of him.

'Jacob.' It was louder this time, full of pain and bitterness. Again he felt the agonising sense of recognition in himself and the certainty that he was somehow responsible for the suffering the speaker was enduring.

'Who are you?' he demanded. 'Tell me your name.'

But the woman ignored his requests. Instead, once again, she began to sob, gently at first but more loudly with every moment that passed. Jacob looked around frantically. Where could he go now to escape the sound?

The sobbing seemed to fill the air as forcibly as the bell that called them to supper every evening. He expected people to come rushing out of doors to see what all the fuss was about. But no one appeared. They had all left for the stone-picking fields. He was alone in a deserted town, tormented by a woman who seemed to blame him for some terrible crime.

A word came into his mind: haunted. And he remembered that this was what ghosts did. They haunted people. Would he be haunted by this woman for the rest of his days? The incessant sound of her sorrow tore at his mind and his body so that he began to feel physically sick. The food he had eaten earlier rose in his gullet and he tasted vomit in his mouth. 'Stop it!' he screamed.

But the sobbing did not stop. Instead, confusingly, it was joined by another noise, which Jacob couldn't recognise at first: a rumbling, humming sound that gradually increased in volume until suddenly he knew what it was. The bus was returning. A moment later it appeared around a bend in the road and came to a halt beside him. Suddenly the sobbing stopped.

With a hissing of air, the doors of the bus flew open. The driver looked in his direction. It was the same woman who had spoken to him the previous day. She smiled sympathetically. 'Missed the bus this morning?' she asked.

Jacob nodded.

'Never mind, I can still take you there. Hop in.'

Without a moment's hesitation, Jacob stepped on board

the bus. Somehow he felt certain that this was the only way he could escape the haunting. The doors closed behind him and the bus pulled away.

'I heard a woman calling my name and sobbing out loud,' Jacob said, as they drove up the hill that led out of the town. 'She wouldn't take any notice of me when I tried to talk to her.'

The driver nodded. 'This town is full of ghosts,' she told him.

'I felt like I knew her,' Jacob said. 'I felt like I recognised her voice. And that seemed to make it worse.'

The driver merely nodded again, as if she had heard the same story many times before.

'Have you ever heard her?' Jacob asked.

She shook her head. 'Everyone hears their own voices,' she replied.

After that she would say no more, despite Jacob's attempts to question her further. In the end he gave up and stared out of the window as the grey buildings of the town gave way to the bleak landscape of the stone-picking fields.

At last they drew up beside the area where the boys from Toby's dormitory were working. After the bus had come to a complete halt, the driver reached behind her for something and handed it to Jacob. He saw that it was a lunch box. He took it gratefully for, of course, he had not brought one from the dining hall.

'You're welcome,' she said.

Berith did not seem surprised that Jacob was late. He just took the lunch box from him and handed over a basket without making any comment, leaving Jacob to wander off and join the others.

'Don't say I told you so,' Jacob said when he found Toby working in a corner by himself.

But Toby was not the sort to crow about being proved right. Instead he looked sympathetic. 'Was it the ghosts?' he asked.

Jacob nodded. 'I could hear someone sobbing,' he said, 'first in the dormitory and then out on the street. I couldn't stand it.'

'Nobody can,' Toby told him.

After that they picked up stones together in silence and, although it was hard work, there was something comforting about it. As he bent down, picked up a stone, straightened up and put it in the basket, time and time again, Jacob found himself wondering about the bus driver. Had she just happened to have a spare lunch box on board? Or had she been expecting to find him in the road, desperate for someone to put him out of his misery? The more he thought about it, the more likely it seemed that she had known he would be there, that she had brought along a spare lunch box in the knowledge that he would be needing one. They are one jump ahead of me all the time, he thought to himself. They already know what I'm going to do next. That needled him. He would have to do much better than this or he would end up like everyone else here, growing used to things.

5. THE GIRL IN THE COURTYARD

Despite his determination not to accept life in Locus, Jacob found the days beginning to slip by without him really noticing. Every morning he got up with the other boys, had breakfast and then took the bus to the stone-picking fields. Every evening he returned, had supper and went to bed.

One night, as he was lying in bed drifting towards sleep, he found himself wondering exactly how many days he had been there and, to his dismay, he realised he was uncertain. Was it thirteen, fourteen or even fifteen? He tried to think of something different that had happened on each day. There was the day he had woken up in the field, the day he had first gone stone-picking, the day he had heard the ghosts, but after that they all began to blur into one.

He tried to differentiate them by thinking of memories that the other boys in the dormitory had spoken of. There was the night that Ivor, a small, pale boy with a slight stutter, had spoken of running down a hill in the snow; then there was the night that Ahmed, a boy with bright eyes and hair that he was always flicking away from his forehead, had spoken of sliding along a polished wooden floor in his socks. But perhaps those had both been on the same night. He couldn't be sure.

He, himself, had not joined in the memory game since the night he had described opening a birthday present, simply because no new memory had come to him. He had listened enviously as other boys described details of the lives they had left behind and he had longed to take part, but days had gone by without any more fragments of his lost world revealing themselves to him. Thinking of this, he fell asleep with a sense of disappointment that was becoming as familiar as the grey uniform he wore each day.

A yellow sun was shining out of a bright blue sky and he was standing in what seemed to be wasteland. There were trees and bushes all around but they looked as if no one had cultivated them, as if they had been allowed to go wild. Some distance away was a wire fence, slightly buckled in one place where someone had obviously climbed over, and on top of this fence a bird was perched. Jacob didn't know what kind of bird it was but it seemed to be looking directly at him out of one beady eye.

As he watched, the bird opened its beak and began to sing. Its song was so perfect that it reached directly into the centre of his being so that he felt as if nothing else mattered. In that moment the thought came to him that the world was a beautiful place and he was glad to be a part of it, a witness to the song of this apparently insignificant creature which nevertheless possessed the power to move him so profoundly. He was aware, at the same time, that this knowledge was an important discovery, and that he needed to act upon it. But he didn't understand what he was supposed to do.

Then he woke up.

The sense of loss that he felt on waking and realising he was lying in bed in the dormitory in Locus was almost overwhelming. The song of the bird and the understanding it had brought drained away from him, like water spilled upon sand. In their place he was left with a deep feeling of emptiness.

Afterwards, he lay awake in the darkness for a long time, listening to the regular breathing of the other boys and wondering what the dream could possibly mean. It was nearly daybreak when sleep finally returned to claim him. This time it was dreamless and when he woke up the following morning he was left with only a confused memory of the vision that had come to him in the depths of the night.

That particular morning happened to be a rest day. On one day out of every seven the boys did not have to go to stone-picking and this was the third such rest day since he had arrived. The first had come when he had been there only three days, the second seven days later and now this one. That meant he had been here seventeen days in all, counting today. So none of his guesses the previous night had been correct. He realised this as he came back from breakfast with Toby. From now on he made up his mind to keep an accurate tally. Perhaps he could carve notches on his bed. He would bring back a sharp stone from the stone-picking fields to do the carving.

As far as he could see, the other boys spent their rest days doing nothing, apart from lying on their beds staring into space, lost in their own thoughts. Perhaps they were bringing to mind the memories they had recalled, polishing them so that they shone brightly like jewels in an empty cupboard. This thought reminded him of his strange dream and he described what he could remember of it to Toby. 'What do you think it means?' he asked.

'It sounds like a memory,' Toby suggested.

'Yes but there was this feeling that went with it, as if the dream was trying to tell me something, but I just couldn't understand it.'

'Perhaps you'll remember more another time.'

Jacob didn't find this reply very satisfying but he knew there was nothing else Toby could say. 'What are you doing today?' he asked.

'Oh nothing much,' Toby replied. 'I'll probably just get some rest.'

They had arrived at the dormitory but Jacob found that he did not want to go inside. The idea of lying on his bed like the other boys and allowing time to trickle past without really noticing it held no attraction for him. 'I think I'll go for a walk,' he said.

There was not much to see in the town, at least not in this part of it. Indeed it would be quite easy to get lost if you went too far. However, he did not intend to go far today. He only wanted to leave behind the familiarity of the dormitory, the rows of boys lying on their beds, each one caught up in a kind of waking dream.

He decided to see what lay beyond the dining hall and set off at a leisurely pace. As he walked, however, he kept a careful eye on the route he took, especially once he had crossed the square and was into unknown territory. It occurred to him that there should be some way of distinguishing between one street and another. Suddenly a picture came into his mind so vividly that it made him stop in his tracks. In the picture he was looking at a wall and on the wall was a street sign. He knew immediately what it was. The name written on the sign was Adelaide Avenue. Jacob repeated the words to himself and he felt sure they held some special meaning for him but, frustratingly, he didn't know what it was. Then the moment passed and the picture dissolved in his mind.

As he resumed his journey, he wondered why there were no street signs here in Locus. They would make it much easier for people to find their way around. But perhaps that was why they were absent. Perhaps those in charge, whoever they were, preferred people to stay in their dormitories as much as possible, because it was easier to control them that way. If so, then they could certainly claim to have been successful for the streets through which Jacob walked were entirely deserted. But perhaps it was less calculated than that, he decided. Perhaps it was simply that the difference between one place and another didn't matter very much in Locus. Everywhere was as drab and insignificant as everywhere else.

As he was thinking this, however, he turned into a little square, formed by the conjunction of four dormitories, and saw that here, at least, an effort had been made to create some kind of atmosphere. In the middle of the square was a great slab of stone in the shape of a cube, twice as tall as Jacob. Against each side of the slab were wooden benches and sitting on one of these was the girl he had noticed on the day he first arrived, the one who had been wearing the red sweater and had stood out like a beacon amid the rows of grey-clothed diners. She looked up and saw him.

'Hello,' she said.

'Hello.'

She was slightly built with jet-black hair and dark golden skin and she looked at him with black eyes behind which he sensed a keen intelligence. 'You arrived on the same day as me, didn't you?' she asked.

Jacob nodded. 'Yes, I think so.' He noticed the familiar two-faced symbol carved in the slab of stone above her head. 'Do you know what that means?' he asked.

She glanced behind her. 'No idea,' she said. 'It seems to be everywhere. Are you going to sit down?'

'OK.'

Feeling slightly self-conscious, he sat down on the bench beside her.

'My name's Aysha,' she told him.

'I'm Jacob.'

'I suppose you woke up in the field, too?'

'Everyone does, as far as I can tell.'

'Can you remember anything from before that?'

Jacob shook his head. 'Not really,' he said, 'except for tiny things.' He told her about opening the present and about looking at a street sign.

'I remember being on a train,' she said.

As she spoke, the image formed itself in Jacob's mind. He could hear the clackety-clack of the train's wheels on the track.

'I was looking out of the window,' she went on.

'What could you see?'

'Houses.'

Jacob closed his eyes to concentrate more fully on the picture she had conjured up. He could see the line of houses, each one distinct from its neighbour in some way, built to a different design perhaps or painted a different colour, their gardens straggling down towards the railway lines, some neatly cultivated, some left to the rule of nature. He was excited by the variety that filled his mind's eye and he longed for Aysha to tell him more but she fell silent. 'Is that it?' he asked.

'That's it.'

He opened his eyes to the reality of Locus again. 'What are the other girls like in your dormitory?' he asked.

'OK,' she replied. 'They're friendly enough but they're a bit . . .' she searched for the right word.

'Used to things?' Jacob suggested.

'Exactly. Sometimes I want to scream at them, to tell you the truth. But it wouldn't do any good.'

'I think it happens to everyone,' Jacob told her. 'Last night I was trying to decide how many days I'd been here and I couldn't remember. I was too tired, I suppose. I worked it out all right this morning but I think that if you stay here long enough you start to accept the way things are.'

'I'm not going to,' Aysha declared. There was a steeliness about her voice as she said this and a light in her eyes that made Jacob feel that perhaps, in her case, it might be true.

'Have you ever thought about trying to escape?' he asked her.

'I think about it every day,' she replied.

'So do I.'

'Why don't we do it together?' she suggested.

'Do you mean that?'

'Of course I mean it.'

'It might not be easy,' Jacob warned. 'They have ways of making you do the things they want you to.'

'What sort of ways?'

He told her about the voice he heard when he had tried to avoid going stone-picking.

'Do you think it really was a ghost?' she asked.

'No I don't,' he said. 'I think they did it, the people who run this place, I mean. I don't know how exactly. It must have been some sort of trick.'

'We'll have to plan our escape carefully,' she told him.

'I agree.'

'Maybe we should spend the next week finding out everything we can about this place,' she went on, 'and what lies beyond it. We can ask everyone in our dormitories what they know. Every scrap of information could be useful.'

'OK.'

'Is it a deal then?' She held out her hand to him and he looked at it, puzzled for a moment. Then he realised what she expected him to do. He took her hand and shook it.

'It's a deal,' he replied.

'Let's meet back here at the same time next week and compare notes,' she suggested. 'Then we can come up with a plan.' She smiled at him when she said this, a smile that was full of real warmth and seemed to light up the grey streets of Locus. For the first time since he had arrived, Jacob began to feel hope stirring inside him.

6. AYSHA'S DREAM

'Do you know anyone who's ever tried to escape from here?' Jacob asked the next day as he and Toby were picking stones together.

'Not really,' Toby replied.

'What do you mean, not really?' Jacob asked. 'Either you do or you don't.'

'Well I did hear about this boy called Calvin who tried to run away but I never met him. I think Stefan might know him.'

'What happened to him?' Jacob asked eagerly.

Toby shrugged. 'He came back,' he said. 'That's all I know.'

It wasn't a very enlightening reply but Jacob did not feel disappointed, not entirely anyway. Where one person has failed, another might succeed, he told himself. He made up his mind to find out more about Calvin.

At lunchtime as they sat on the ground eating, Jacob got up and went over to Stefan. Stefan was always by himself but this was not because the other boys disliked him. In fact they all seemed to have a certain amount of respect for him. It was just that on the whole he preferred his own company. He never looked for conversation with anyone else, nor did he encourage it when others sought him out. True to form, he took absolutely no notice as Jacob sat down beside him.

'I hear you know a boy called Calvin,' Jacob began.

'I've met him, that's all,' Stefan replied.

'Toby tells me he tried to escape.'

'So they say.'

'Do you know what happened to him?'

Stefan shook his head. 'He ran away, he came back. That's all I know.'

Jacob could see that it wasn't going to be easy finding out anything from Stefan. But he wasn't prepared to give up that easily. 'What sort of a person is he?' he asked.

'A fool,' Stefan said.

'Why do you say that?'

'Because anyone who goes wandering off into the wilderness without any idea where he's going is a fool.'

As always, when he talked to Stefan, Jacob felt a tide of frustration rising inside him. 'Don't you think it might be worth at least trying to get out of here?' he asked.

'Look around you,' Stefan said. 'What do you see on the ground?'

'Rocks,' Jacob said.

'Exactly.' Stefan looked back at him smugly, as if Jacob's answer was proof of something.

'So what's your point?' Jacob demanded.

'My point is that if there's a river behind you and nothing but rocks in front, then maybe the best thing to do is to stay put.' He sat there, looking pleased with himself.

Jacob felt the urge to grab him and shake him but he

resisted it. For one thing Stefan was much bigger than he was. But it was not just that. It was that he sensed there was a hidden motivation behind Stefan's pig-headedness, as if he had his own reasons for refusing to think about whatever lay beyond the narrow world of Locus. 'Why are you like this?' he asked.

A peculiar look came over Stefan's face. 'Why are any of us like we are?' he said. 'That's a question we can't answer, isn't it? Because none of us have enough information.'

Momentarily, Jacob was lost for words. He wanted to say something that would really make an impact on Stefan, something that would penetrate beneath his armour, but he couldn't think of the words. As he sat there, racking his brain, Berith came out of his hut and shambled over towards them. 'Lunchtime's over,' he called out in his harsh, cracked voice.

'Time to pick up some more stones,' Stefan said, getting to his feet.

'Enjoy yourself,' Jacob told him, bitterly. He, too, got up and walked over to where Berith was waiting to take their empty lunch boxes.

'Did you learn anything?' Toby asked, when they had resumed work.

'Yes,' Jacob replied. 'I learned that you can't crack a rock with your fingers.'

Over the course of the next few days, Jacob spoke to every boy in his dormitory and asked them what they knew about Locus, the people who ran the place and what lay beyond. Everyone other than Stefan was willing to tell him whatever they knew but this didn't amount to much. Nobody knew how big Locus was. Most people agreed that it stretched along the bank of the river for a very long way. Ivor, the boy with the stutter, insisted that it went on for ever. 'That isn't possible,' Jacob pointed out. 'It has to end somewhere.'

Ivor shook his head. 'The streets full of dormitories never s-s-stop,' he insisted.

Ahmed, who was Ivor's friend, laughed out loud. 'Don't take any notice of him,' he told Jacob. 'He's full of crazy ideas. He thinks everybody in the world is going to end up here.'

'It's true,' Ivor said, nodding his head eagerly. 'That's why we have to keep clearing the f-f-fields. To make room.'

Ahmed raised his eyebrows and smiled at Jacob in a way that showed what he thought of his friend's theory.

Afterwards, Jacob lay on his bed and thought about what Ivor had said. He couldn't believe in a town that spread out for ever, nor did he seriously think for one moment that everybody in the world would end up in Locus. That was just nonsense. But one thing was clear: Locus was expanding all the time. That was why they were clearing the fields of stones, after all, so that new dormitories could be built. No doubt more and more people were waking up in the field each day with no memory of how they had got there. And as far as he could see, that was the sole purpose of Locus. It was a place where the lost were gathered together. There was no other reason for its existence. Nothing took place there except for eating, sleeping and the daily trip to the stone-fields.

Yet the scraps of memory that the boys in his dormitory had recovered had not been like this. They had offered glimpses of an entirely different world, a world full of colour and vitality. And Jacob wanted that many-coloured world back. He sighed. The more he thought about it, the more frustrated he became. It was like running into a wall over and over again.

By the time the next rest day arrived Jacob was looking forward to meeting Aysha and finding out what she had learned. He hoped that she would have gathered more information than he had. There was something very purposeful about her, something that suggested she was not someone who wasted time. If anyone could show him the way out of Locus, Jacob suspected that it would be Aysha.

'Are you going for another of your walks?' Toby asked that morning as they strolled back from the dining hall.

'Yes.'

'Where do you go?'

'Oh nowhere in particular,' Jacob replied. For some reason he didn't want to tell Toby about Aysha, not just yet anyway. It might mean telling him about their plan to run away together and then Toby might say something discouraging. He wouldn't mean to. It would just come out. He would make some remark and then suddenly the whole thing would start to look impossible. So Jacob's reply was deliberately vague. 'I just wander around,' he said.

'But what's there to see? It's all the same, isn't it?' Toby asked.

'Not quite,' Jacob told him. 'There are one or two little

places of interest. I found a square with some benches in the middle.'

'Benches?'

'Yeah, you know, to sit on.'

'You can sit in the dormitory,' said Toby.

'I prefer to sit outside sometimes. It makes a change.'

They had reached the dormitory now and the time had come to part company. 'Well enjoy your walk,' Toby said. 'I don't think I'll bother to come with you.' He went inside.

Jacob followed the same route he had taken the week before, crossing the great square and passing through a series of little streets until he found himself in the smaller square with the stone cube. He saw that Aysha had got there ahead of him and was sitting at the same spot. He waved as he walked towards her.

She did not wave back and he knew immediately that something was wrong. Her face had lost its eager look. Instead she seemed utterly dejected. 'Are you all right?' he asked.

She opened her mouth to speak but her bottom lip began to tremble and her eyes filled up with tears. Then she covered her face with her hands and wept.

'What's the matter?' he asked, sitting down beside her. It occurred to him that he ought to put his arm round her, but a feeling of uncertainty stopped him.

'I'm sorry,' she said, making an effort to pull herself together.

'Has something bad happened?'

She nodded her head.

'Tell me about it.'

Aysha bit her lip. 'I had a dream,' she said.

Jacob looked at her in surprise. Was that all? He had expected something much more serious.

'I dreamt about my mother,' she went on.

He felt a stab of envy. He would dearly have liked to dream about his own mother but he could not even conjure up an image of her face. 'What was she doing?' he asked.

'She was in a room sitting on a bed. I remember noticing that the wall behind her was half painted as if someone had been in the middle of decorating it and then had lost interest. Actually I think it was my bedroom, though I don't know why I felt that. Anyway, she was sitting on the bed, staring at something she held in her hand and her eyes were full of tears and I could see that she was really upset. At first I couldn't tell what she was staring at but then I seemed to be looking through her eyes and I saw it was a photograph of a girl and I realised that the girl was me.' She paused and looked at Jacob.

'Is that it?' he asked. He could see why the dream had upset her but it still seemed to him that her reaction was a bit extreme.

She shook her head. 'No. There's more. After a little while my mother spoke and it was as if she was speaking to the girl in the photograph, to me, I mean.'

'What did she say?'

Aysha hesitated. Her face was completely white and Jacob thought for a moment she might faint. But then she took a deep breath and spoke. 'These are the exact words my mother said: Oh Aysha why did you have to die?'

'Well I suppose that's what she thinks,' Jacob said.

'I mean it must be what all our parents think. We've just disappeared, haven't we? And they probably . . .'

'No Jacob,' she said, holding up her hand to interrupt him. 'You don't understand.' She turned her dark brown eyes on Jacob's and it seemed to him they were filled with horror. 'I've been thinking about it ever since I woke up and about the reason we can't remember how we got here.' Her voice had been getting quieter and quieter as she said this. Now she leaned closer to him and spoke in a whisper. 'There's only one explanation that really makes sense. We're dead, Jacob.'

7. THE OTHER SIDE

Jacob stared at her in amazement. He couldn't believe what she had just suggested. 'We can't be dead,' he said. 'I mean, we're standing here having a conversation. We couldn't be doing that if we were dead.'

Aysha shrugged. 'Maybe this is what happens after you die, maybe you go into another world and this is it.'

A dizziness took hold of Jacob as the implications of what she was saying began to sink in. He put his hand to his head, as if to steady himself. 'Wait a minute! What evidence have you got for this idea?' he demanded. 'Apart from your dream, I mean?'

'None really,' Aysha said, 'except for the voices.'

'What voices?'

'The voices people hear when they refuse to go stone-picking. You told me that you heard them yourself.'

'I heard someone sobbing and calling out my name,' Jacob agreed. 'But I don't see how that proves I'm dead.'

'People say they're ghosts, don't they?'

'Yes.'

'Well after I had that dream I suddenly thought: what if they're not ghosts at all. What if we're the ghosts?'

'I don't know what you're talking about,' Jacob said. He

felt a surge of irritation. How could she be talking such nonsense? And what had happened to the brave, optimistic, determined girl of the week before?

'What I'm trying to say is this,' Aysha went on. 'Maybe what people hear are the voices of the living, the people who've been left behind, the ones who are mourning for us.'

As she said this, Jacob suddenly remembered how the woman who had called his name had seemed to blame him for her sorrow. Quickly he pushed the thought to the back of his mind. 'I don't want to listen to any more of this,' he said. 'It's just stupid.' He stood up abruptly and walked away, leaving her sitting in the square by herself. He refused to look back.

'What's the matter with everyone?' he asked himself as he strode angrily back to the dormitory. They all seemed determined to give up without a fight. He had really believed in Aysha. He'd been so sure that she wouldn't be like the others. Well, he'd been wrong about that. Still, that didn't mean he had to join her, did it? Even if he was the only one in the whole place to put up a resistance, he would keep on. He shook his head in despair. 'Dead!' he muttered to himself. 'What a stupid thing to say!'

The other boys were all lying or sitting on their beds when Jacob got back. Something about the way they looked, as if they were all half-asleep, infuriated him all over again. Suddenly making up his mind to have it out with them, he stood in the middle of the room and raised his voice. 'There's something I want to talk to you all about,' he said.

They sat up and regarded him with curiosity, all except Stefan who remained flat on his back with his eyes closed, though Jacob knew perfectly well he wasn't asleep.

'I've just been talking to a girl who arrived here on the same day as me,' Jacob went on. 'She told me about a dream she'd had. I want you all to hear it.' He described Aysha's dream and then told them about the conclusion she had drawn. 'She actually thinks we're all dead,' he said. 'Can you believe that?' He studied their faces, expecting them to show complete disdain for such a ridiculous idea, hoping that someone would burst out laughing or make some mocking comment. But to his dismay he saw several of them nodding gravely as if this confirmed what they had long believed privately. No one spoke.

'Well, isn't anybody going to say anything?' he demanded.

Stefan opened his eyes and propped himself up on one elbow. 'What do you want us to say?' he asked in his familiar lazy drawl that suggested he found the whole discussion rather a waste of time.

'I want you to tell me that you don't agree with her of course, that you think it's nonsense, that she's just a crazy girl who's had a bad dream and I shouldn't listen to her.'

Stefan made a gesture with his hand, as if he were humouring a child. 'OK, if that's what you want to believe,' he said.

Jacob glared back at him. 'I'm not talking about what I want to believe,' he said. 'I'm talking about the truth.' He could feel the tension rising as all his anger and frustration began to focus upon Stefan.

'We don't know the truth though, do we?' another voice said. It was Toby's. He had got up from his bed and come over to where Jacob was standing. Now he put a reassuring hand on Jacob's shoulder but Jacob shrugged it off angrily.

'You too?' he said. 'You lot sicken me!' he shouted. 'You act as if it wouldn't make any difference if we were dead.'

'Well would it?' Stefan asked him. He stared challengingly at Jacob. He spoke softly but his voice had a hard edge to it, as if he was prepared to meet Jacob word for word.

'Of course it would,' Jacob told him. 'Because if we're not dead, if we've just been brought here to work, for example, if we've been . . . whatever the word is . . .'

'K-k-kidnapped,' Ivor volunteered.

'Yes, thank you,' Jacob said, turning to him and nodding gratefully. 'If we've just been kidnapped, like Ivor says, then there's always a chance that we can escape, get out of here and go back home. But if we are dead then there's no hope at all, is there?'

'Here we go again,' Stefan said, wearily.

'What's that supposed to mean?' Jacob demanded.

'It means that you're always talking about home as if it was so absolutely bloody marvellous,' Stefan said, 'when the truth is you can't remember anything about it.' He was looking at Jacob as he said this with an expression that was impossible to fathom. 'None of you can,' he went on, 'even though you play your silly little memory game every night. Well let me tell you something. I remember my home much better than any of you. And I'm not talking about tiny details like kicking a ball.'

'I thought you couldn't remember anything at all,' Jacob said in surprise.

'Did I ever say that? Did I? Listen! Just because I don't join in with your game, doesn't mean I don't recall what happened. I can remember all sorts of stuff about my home and you know what? None of it was nice and cosy, like you seem to imagine everybody's home must be. I can remember getting hit every time I opened my mouth. There was nothing very pleasant about that.'

He paused and there was complete silence in the room. All eyes were fixed on him. 'I can remember some terrible things,' he continued, 'things I don't want to remember. So do me a favour will you? Just stop rocking the boat because some of us are perfectly all right as we are.'

Jacob looked at him for a long time. He could think of nothing to say in reply. Finally he walked slowly over to his own bed and lay down. He felt as if some thick, heavy substance was congealing inside him. Then he realised what it was: despair. After a while tears began trickling down his face and he made no attempt to brush them away.

Over the next few days a mood of grim acceptance settled over Jacob. He made no further attempts to discuss the situation with any of the others. There was no point, he could see that now. They all believed they were dead. They had probably believed it for a long time but none of them had wanted to put it into words. He told himself they were

63

all fools, that they would rather believe they were dead than face the difficulty of trying to escape from the trap in which they'd been caught. He utterly refused to accept the idea himself. It was nonsense, complete rubbish. It was just what the people who ran Locus wanted them to believe, so that they didn't cause any trouble. And yet the more he assured himself of this, the less convinced he became.

It was at night that he reached his lowest point. During the day it was possible to put gloomy thoughts to the back of his mind, to focus on whatever task he had in hand. Getting dressed, washing, eating his breakfast, collecting his lunch box, climbing aboard the bus, picking up stones – all the routine tasks of his life in this community of lost souls served as distractions from the doubts which now began to gnaw away at this certainty. But at night there was nothing else to do except lie awake in the darkness and wonder whether perhaps it wasn't true after all. Could this be what death was like?

His attitude towards Locus began to change. He no longer spent his time trying to plan how he might escape. Instead he simply went from day to day, sinking deeper inside himself until he scarcely spoke to anyone. One morning when they were sitting down to breakfast together, Toby turned to him and said, 'Come on Jacob, cheer up! It's not that bad.'

Jacob looked at him in amazement. 'Cheer up!' he said. 'Cheer up! What exactly is there to be cheerful about?'

Toby shrugged. 'Friendship?' he suggested.

The indignation which had boiled up inside Jacob at

Toby's words died. 'Sorry,' he said. 'You're right. It's just, you know, there's not much to look forward to, is there?'

'I've been thinking,' Toby said.

'About what?'

'About your friend Aysha's dream.'

'What about it?'

'Well the thing is, maybe we are dead and maybe we aren't, I don't know.'

'But you believe we are, don't you?' Jacob asked.

Toby hesitated for a moment, then he nodded. 'Yes, I do,' he said. 'I suppose I'd already come to that conclusion even before you stood up in the middle of the room and made your announcement. But that's not what I wanted to talk to you about. Well not just that, anyway. See, I've been here for longer than you have and that means I've been remembering things for longer than you. And one of the things I remembered about was ghosts.'

'What about them?'

'Well for a start I remembered what they are.'

'They're dead people who come back to life,' Jacob said. 'You already told me that.'

Toby shook his head. 'That's not strictly true,' he said. 'I think it would be more accurate to say that they are the spirits of the dead.'

The word 'spirits' was unrecognisable to Jacob and yet it seemed to drop into his mind like a stone falling into water. Ripples of half-understood meaning spread out from it and disappeared into an immense lake of memory, a lake whose depths remained dark and mysterious even while its surface was troubled. 'What does that mean?' he asked.

'I think it means that when a person dies, not everything is gone,' Toby told him. 'Something is left over, a kind of force that outlasts the body. That's the spirit.'

Jacob considered this. He thought he understood what Toby was getting at. 'So are you trying to say that we're spirits?' he asked. 'Because I don't see how that can be true. We've got bodies, haven't we? I mean, when I wake up after a hard day's stone-picking it's my body that hurts.'

'I know,' Toby said. 'I'm not suggesting that we're spirits. But I think that if we are dead, we've moved on somehow and it must be our spirits that have moved.'

Jacob shook his head. 'I don't understand,' he said. 'You seem to be contradicting yourself.'

'I'm not sure I understand, either,' Toby replied, 'at least not completely. But what I thought was this: if we are dead, if we have moved on to another world, then in this new world we're just as real as we were in the old one. So maybe we're alive in this world but dead in the one we left behind.'

'So where does that get us?' Jacob asked. It was hard to see how Toby's odd ideas were any kind of help.

'Wait a minute,' Toby said. 'There's something else that I remembered, something more important. It came to me yesterday when we were stone-picking. I remembered being round at another boy's house one night. It was late and there were several other boys there. I think it might have been somebody's birthday and we were all staying the night. We were in the sort of mood where you're ready to do anything for a laugh.'

Jacob immediately began to picture the scene. He

imagined a group of boys of about his own age. He could feel the sense of excitement they felt at being together, on their own, late at night, able to do things that they weren't normally allowed to do, and get away with them.

'We were all sitting around a table,' Toby went on, 'and we were holding hands. One boy was laughing and the others kept telling him to be quiet. Then we all closed our eyes.'

Jacob could still see the picture clearly but he couldn't quite understand what was going on. 'What were you doing?' he asked.

'Trying to contact the dead,' Toby told him.

Jacob felt a shiver run up his spine. 'What do you mean?' he asked.

'Just what I say,' Toby told him. 'I even remembered the word for what we were trying to do. It's called a séance.'

The blood in Jacob's veins seemed to quicken at the very mention of the word. He still did not understand but something told him that what Toby was describing was extremely important. 'Did you succeed?' he demanded.

'I don't know,' Toby said, to Jacob's enormous disappointment. 'I don't remember any more. I've got a feeling that we didn't, because no one would take it seriously enough. But that's not really the point.'

'What is the point?' Jacob asked. He felt frustrated, filled with a sense that some vital discovery was within his grasp, but confused about exactly what it was.

Toby did not seem to share his agitation. He continued speaking as calmly as if he were explaining to Jacob where he should put his dirty cutlery after the meal. 'Well I just thought that if the living could contact the dead,' he said, 'then why can't we do things the other way round? Why can't we hold our own séance and see if we can contact the living?' He looked uncertainly at Jacob. 'What do you think?'

This was what Jacob had been waiting for. He did not hesitate. 'We have to do it,' he said.

8. MAKING CONTACT

The first thing Jacob wanted to do was tell Aysha about Toby's suggestion. He wasn't quite sure why he felt this urge so strongly, but he did. Perhaps it was the thought of the way she had sat beside him with her head in her hands, quietly weeping. Or perhaps it was because, now that he had cheered up a little, he felt an aftertaste of guilt about the way he had stormed off, leaving her alone with her misery.

However, no sooner had he decided on this than he realised he didn't know how to find her. They had made no further arrangements to meet in the square and he had no idea which dormitory she lived in. There was nothing else for it – he would have to try to find her when everyone assembled in the dining hall to eat.

This proved more difficult than he had expected. The first time he'd spotted her she had stood out because of the red sweater she'd been wearing but, like himself, she had long ago exchanged her own clothes for the grey uniform worn by all the residents of Locus. Now she would merge into the background like all the others.

As he studied the faces of the diners that evening, he thought about Ivor's theory that everybody in the world would eventually come to live in Locus. Perhaps it was not so ridiculous after all. There were hundreds of children in this hall and Toby had assured him that there were many, many more dining halls, if you could be bothered to explore the length and breadth of Locus.

He began wandering around the dining hall scanning faces at random. But after a while he saw that this was hopeless. He could not even be sure which tables he had checked and which he had not. He decided to approach the problem systematically, starting at one end of the room and working his way back and forth. But even this was not foolproof because people were coming and going all the time. Discouraged by the enormity of the task, he was on the point of giving up altogether when he caught sight of a girl sitting a little apart from the others, eating slowly, almost solemnly. He looked more closely. It was definitely Aysha but her appearance seemed to have changed subtly since he had first seen her. As she looked up and caught sight of him, he realised that she looked older, less like a child and more like an adult. He sat down beside her.

'How are you?' he asked.

She gave him a look that suggested she thought this an unnecessary question.

'Sorry I walked off like that last time we met,' Jacob said. He had not intended to begin with an apology but somehow he found himself coming out with it.

Her face brightened a little. 'That's all right,' she said.

'I've been thinking about what you said,' Jacob went on, 'and I've decided you might be right.' Once again, he surprised himself by this admission. He hadn't even told

Toby what he really thought, even when agreeing to the séance. But Aysha seemed to have an effect on him that he did not quite understand, so that he found himself having to be entirely truthful when he spoke to her.

'Is that why you came to talk to me?' she asked.

'Partly,' Jacob agreed, 'but mainly for another reason. A friend of mine called Toby came up with an idea this morning. I wanted to tell you about it.' He went on to explain.

Aysha listened intently. After Jacob had finished, he noticed that her expression had regained a little of its earlier eagerness. 'Can you take me to meet your friend?' she asked.

'All right.'

They made their way back to Toby. After they had been introduced, Aysha quizzed Toby about his memory of the séance. She wanted to know every tiny detail – exactly how they had held hands, who had spoken and what words had been said.

Toby shook his head. 'I can't remember everything,' he said. 'You know what it's like with these flashes of memory. They're very vivid but extremely short.'

'You have no idea whether it was successful?' Aysha asked.

'I don't think it was. I think we were just messing about.'

Aysha looked disappointed. 'So the whole thing was just a joke?' she asked.

'Yes, but I still think it could work,' Toby insisted.

'Why?'

'Because I remember very clearly how I felt at the time.

It's hard to describe but I had the feeling there was something very daring about what we were doing, that it was something we shouldn't really have been doing at all, a bit like playing with fire.'

Aysha nodded.

'I felt as if what we were trying to do was real enough,' Toby explained, 'and, to be honest, I wasn't sure I wanted to succeed because I was a bit frightened of what might happen.'

'How do you feel about trying it again, the other way round?' Aysha asked.

'Nervous,' Toby admitted, 'but I think Jacob's right – we have to try.'

'Where should we do it?' Jacob asked, keen to get on to the planning stage.

'What's wrong with your dormitory?' Aysha suggested.

'Nothing,' Jacob said. 'It's just that not everyone there might approve.'

'Are you thinking of Stefan?' Toby asked.

'Yes.'

'He won't interfere,' Toby said. 'He'll probably make a few sarcastic remarks, that's all. Just don't take any notice of him.'

'So when are we going to do it?' Aysha asked.

Toby shrugged. 'Whenever you like,' he said.

'What about tomorrow night?' Aysha suggested.

'All right.'

They discussed the arrangements for a little while longer. Despite the fact that the séance had been Toby's idea, it was agreed that Jacob would explain it to the rest of the boys. 'You're better at that sort of thing than me,' Toby told him. 'You're more of a leader.'

This surprised Jacob. He would never have thought of himself as a leader. He wasn't big or strong, like Stefan. All he knew about himself was that he disliked being told what to do. In fact whenever anyone, like Berith for example, issued him with a direct order, he felt an instinctive desire to do the opposite. Perhaps he'd had his fill of being told what to do when he was alive. This thought occurred to him as he and Toby walked back to the dormitory together.

He wasted no time in explaining the idea to the others. They all seemed quite keen, except for Stefan of course. He took absolutely no notice of the suggestion, simply lying on his bed with his eyes closed.

'What time will we do it?' Ahmed asked.

'After we've eaten,' Jacob said, 'when everybody's got back here.'

'Do you think it will w-w-work?' Ivor asked.

'I don't know,' Jacob said. 'We'll have to see.' But afterwards, as he was getting ready for bed, the thought came to him that in a way it had already worked. Only a day earlier he had been in a state of profound depression. He had given up even thinking about the world he had left behind. Now his hope had reignited and once again his will was focused on the land of the living.

Despite Toby's assertion that Jacob was a natural leader, it was actually Aysha who took charge of things the following evening. It was strange to see a girl in the dormitory. Even though she was dressed in the same grey uniform as the rest of them, she stood out and Jacob was aware of the other boys staring at her. For some reason it made him feel protective. She was his friend and he did not want anyone saying anything to her that might be interpreted as hostile. But, in fact, everyone seemed prepared to like her and, more importantly, to allow her to organise them into forming a circle on the floor, everyone except Stefan, that is. He sat on his bed and watched them with an air of amusement. 'Well at least this is something different,' he said.

'You should join in,' Aysha told him. She was sitting directly opposite him, in between Jacob and Toby.

'I don't think I'll bother,' he said. 'I'll just watch the fun from here.'

Aysha shrugged. 'Please yourself,' she said. 'It's your loss.'

Now that they were all seated and holding hands, the atmosphere in the dormitory was not unlike Toby's description of his memory. It was as if they were all having fun in a slightly illicit way, doing something that those in authority would not have approved of, something daring and rather dangerous.

'How are we going to begin?' Jacob asked. He was conscious that his voice sounded slightly nervous.

'I've thought about that,' Aysha said. From the confident way she spoke it seemed that she did not share his unease. 'I've prepared some words to say,' she went on, 'not a great big speech but just a sort of introduction, unless either of you want to do it.'

'No, you go ahead,' Jacob replied and Toby nodded in agreement.

'It's a pity we can't dim the lights,' Aysha said, 'but never mind. Can everybody close their eyes please. And no talking.'

It felt very strange sitting on the floor of the dormitory holding Toby's and Aysha's hands, but Jacob knew it was important to take this whole exercise seriously. He tried to let his mind float in the way Toby had advised when he had first begun stone-picking.

Aysha began to speak in a tone quite unlike her usual manner. Her voice was surprisingly deep and sonorous, almost a chant and the words seemed to resonate in the air around them. 'We, the dead, are assembled here this night,' she began, 'to join our minds together and to send our thoughts across the barrier between this world and the world of the living. We wish to make contact with those we have left behind. If there is anybody there who would like to speak to us, will they please do so now.'

There was a long silence. Jacob felt a strong desire to open his eyes but he resisted the temptation. After a while Aysha repeated her speech but again there was no response.

'It isn't working,' one of the boys muttered.

'Of course it isn't working,' said Stefan's voice derisively.

Jacob opened his eyes and let go of the hands he was holding. He saw that most of the others had their eyes open, too, and they were all looking in Stefan's direction.

'And I'll tell you something else,' Stefan went on. 'It's not going to work. You can sit there all night long with your eyes shut, talking to nobody, if that's what makes you happy. But you won't get any answer.'

Anger welled up in Jacob. 'Why don't you shut up?' he said.

'Because I don't feel like it,' Stefan replied, with his usual irritating smugness.

'Do you know what I think?' Aysha said suddenly. 'I think Stefan really wants to join us.'

Stefan laughed. 'No I don't,' he said. 'That's a ridiculous thing to say.'

'Oh but I think you do,' Aysha said, adopting an oddly teasing tone. 'It's just that you're frightened to commit yourself. Isn't that the truth?'

'I'm not frightened of anything,' Stefan said. The curtness of his reply suggested she had nettled him.

'Then join us, if you're not scared,' Aysha said. 'If it doesn't mean anything to you, it can't hurt can it? Or are you someone who likes to hide behind talk?'

'I don't hide behind anything,' Stefan said. He sounded angry now.

'So prove it,' Aysha told him.

There was a moment's silence. Aysha continued to look directly at Stefan, challenging him with her gaze. Stefan stared hostilely back. But to Jacob's surprise, it was Stefan who broke first. 'All right then,' he said, standing up. 'If it matters so much to you, I'll show you that your little game doesn't bother me in the least.' He walked over to the circle, sitting down between Ahmed and Ivor.

'Good,' Aysha said. 'Is everybody ready?'

There were murmurs of assent.

'Then please join hands, close your eyes and concentrate.'

They did as she told them and she began to repeat her speech inviting the living to make contact with them. Almost immediately Jacob sensed that something was different. As Aysha spoke, the air around him seemed to thicken and he felt a sense of weightlessness take hold of him. The walls and floor of the room began to recede and he felt as if he were floating in some unknown element that was simultaneously outside and inside him. By now Aysha's voice seemed to be coming from a very long way off and he could no longer make out clearly what she was saying. Instead his attention was captured by a point of light floating directly in front of him. The more he focused on this point of light the further away it seemed to be and yet at the same time it was growing larger. Then he realised that he was looking down the length of an enormous tunnel. No, not just looking down a tunnel but travelling down it at enormous speed, so fast in fact that he began to feel dreadfully sick and desperate for the sensation to stop.

And suddenly it did.

Like a cork being pulled from a bottle, he emerged at the end of the tunnel, to find himself standing in a room, a room which he immediately recognised as the living room of his house. And there in front of him were his parents. His father was standing in the middle of the room and his mother was sitting on a chair looking at him. Joy and relief welled up in him so strongly that it felt like pain. 'Mum! Dad!' he shouted.

They took absolutely no notice of him.

'Look I'm sorry but I can't go on like this any longer,' his father said. It was clear that he and Jacob's mother were having an argument.

'It's me!' Jacob yelled, interrupting.

But neither of them turned their heads to look in his direction. His father went on speaking in a low voice, his words steeped in bitterness. 'I know you blame me for Jacob's death,' he said.

Jacob had been about to walk over and stand in between them but these words stopped him in his tracks. So it was true. He was dead. Along with this thought came the realisation that they could not see him. They were not ignoring him. He simply wasn't there as far as they were concerned.

'You're wrong,' his mother replied. 'I don't blame you. If you want to know the truth, I blame myself.' Her voice sounded full of a barely controlled anger, an anger that had nothing on which to focus. 'I should have known where he was going and what he was doing. But I didn't. I was too busy with my own life.'

His father shook his head. 'It's no good thinking like that,' he said. 'We've got to try to put this behind us.'

His mother stood up, frowning furiously, her rage now directing itself against her husband. 'How can I put it behind me?' she demanded. 'I don't know how you can even say that!'

'Because it's destroying our relationship,' his father said. Tentatively, he reached out to touch her but she brushed his hand away.

Jacob continued to watch this miserable drama unfolding before him. All the pleasure he had felt on seeing his parents again had drained away. Instead he felt horrified at the way they were behaving, and at the same time utterly powerless to do anything.

'I think we should spend some time apart,' his mother said.

His father looked at her for a long time. Then he sighed. 'Is that what you really want?' he asked.

'I think it might be for the best.'

'No, Mum!' Jacob cried out. 'Don't do this!' But it was no good. She could not hear him. A moment later he found himself being sucked backwards away from the scene. Once again he experienced the sensation of travelling through a tunnel at terrifying speed. Once again he felt certain that he would be sick at any moment. Then, suddenly, it was all over. He opened his eyes and found himself back in the dormitory.

The others were all staring at him in obvious astonishment. 'Are you all right?' Aysha asked.

Jacob nodded. 'I think so,' he said.

'What on earth was all that about?' Toby asked. 'You were shouting your head off.'

Jacob looked at him in surprise. 'Didn't anything happen to you?' he asked.

Toby shook his head. 'I was just sitting there with my eyes closed, waiting for something to happen, when all of a sudden you started shouting.'

'Didn't anybody else see anything?' Jacob demanded. He looked around the circle.

They all shook their heads. Even Stefan seemed subdued by what had happened. His usual sardonic manner had deserted him and he looked at Jacob with an air of distinct curiosity.

'I saw my parents,' Jacob told them. 'They were having a quarrel. About me. About my death.'

'You don't think you just made it up?' a boy called James asked. Blond-haired and pale-faced, he was normally one of the quietest boys in the dormitory and for that reason Jacob answered him calmly. If anyone else had put the same question to him, he might have shouted at them. But there was always something polite, almost respectful about James.

'I didn't make it up,' Jacob said, 'and it wasn't a dream, before you ask. It really happened. I saw my parents, they were discussing my death.' He turned to Aysha. 'You were right all the time,' he said. 'I'm sorry.'

'It doesn't matter,' she said, graciously.

'At least now you know the truth,' Stefan said. For once he was not crowing. Instead, he spoke mildly, almost sympathetically. 'You'll find that makes it easier to accept this place. You'll be able to settle down now.'

To his surprise, Stefan's comments did not anger Jacob. Instead they seemed to confirm a sense of absolute certainty that had been growing inside him. 'That's where you're wrong,' he said, shaking his head, 'because this makes it even more important that I don't just accept the situation. Don't you see? I've got to do something about it. Otherwise my parents are going to split up. I can't let that happen.'

Stefan gave him a pitying look. 'There isn't anything you can do about it,' he said. 'You're dead. End of story. Your parents are going to have to sort out their problems by themselves. Maybe you don't remember this but I can promise you one thing: nobody comes back from the dead.'

There was silence after he spoke and Jacob could feel them all looking at him, waiting for him to accept the inevitable but he shook his head. 'Well I intend to try,' he said.

9. CALVIN'S STORY

Sitting on the bus the next morning, Jacob asked Stefan if he would introduce him to Calvin. Stefan looked at him for a long time before answering. Finally he said, 'You know one day, not long after I first got here, I was lying on my bed thinking about nothing in particular when I saw this weird-looking insect. It was trying to climb up the wall beside the door and it kept getting about this high.' He held up his hand and indicated the distance with his thumb and second finger. 'Then it would fall off. But each time it fell off, it would start all over again.' He paused and Jacob realised that he was waiting for some sort of response.

'So what happened in the end?' Jacob asked. 'Did it get to the top?'

Stefan shook his head. 'James came through the door and stepped on it,' he said.

'OK,' Jacob said, 'I get your point but I still want to meet up with Calvin. Will you arrange it or not?'

Stefan shrugged. 'If you insist,' he said.

'I do.'

The meeting took place that evening. Stefan led the way to Calvin's dormitory a little uncertainly, stopping several times and once turning back in the direction they had just come. But at last he came to a halt outside a dormitory identical to their own. 'Are you sure this is the right one?' Jacob asked.

'Of course I'm not sure,' Stefan said curtly. 'They all look the same, don't they? Anyway, we'll soon find out. But listen, before we go in: Calvin is a bit strange, OK? He looks like he's half-asleep but he's very sharp and he doesn't like people asking stupid questions. Got it?'

Jacob nodded.

Like the door to their own dormitory, this one was not locked. Stefan pushed it open and they stepped inside. He glanced round at the occupants, then made his way over to a bed in the far corner of the room where a very tall, skinny boy with copper-coloured skin and tight black curly hair sat hugging his knees. He had his head on one side and he was humming tunelessly to himself. As they drew level he stopped humming and looked them up and down.

Jacob saw immediately that Calvin had a presence about him that put even Stefan on the defensive. He took his time before speaking and when he spoke it was in a lazy but confident voice. 'How's it going, Stefan?' he asked.

'Not bad, Calvin,' Stefan said. 'How about you?'

Calvin spread his hands wide. 'I get along,' he said. He swung his legs off the bed. 'Who's your shadow?' he asked, jerking his head to indicate Jacob.

'His name's Jacob,' Stefan said. 'He's in my dormitory. He wants to talk to you.'

Calvin pursed his lips, as if deciding whether or not he wanted to talk to Jacob. Finally he said, 'You'd better sit down then.'

Stefan perched on the edge of the bed and Jacob sat on the floor nearby.

'So what do you want to talk about, Jacob?' Calvin asked. The question sounded friendly enough but there was something about the way he said it that suggested he might not cooperate with Jacob's inquiry so easily, if it didn't suit him.

'I wanted to ask you about the time you tried to escape from here,' Jacob told him.

Calvin nodded, as if he had expected this. 'What do you want to know about it?' he asked.

'Everything,' Jacob said.

Calvin raised his eyebrows. 'Everything,' he said. 'That's quite a request.'

'Well, first of all I wanted to know what made you decide to do it,' Jacob suggested.

Calvin raised one hand to indicate the rest of the dormitory. 'Look around you,' he said. 'You see any good reason to stay here?'

'The others haven't tried to escape, though,' Jacob pointed out.

'Because they're too scared, that's why,' Calvin told him.

'You're not scared, then?'

Calvin gazed levelly back at him. 'Do I look as if I scare easily?' he asked.

'No,' Jacob agreed.

'Next question,' Calvin said.

'Where were you heading?'

'The Palace of Remembrance,' Calvin replied. 'Where else?'

'The Palace of Remembrance?' Jacob repeated. 'What's that?'

Calvin looked at Stefan. 'Your friend doesn't know very much,' he said.

'He hasn't been here long,' Stefan told him, apologetically. He turned to Jacob. 'It's a story that people tell each other around here,' he said. 'They say that if you go to the end of the stone-picking fields and carry on in the direction of the setting sun for three days you come to a stone palace where the king and queen of this land live.'

'Is it true?' Jacob asked.

'We never found it, that's for sure,' Calvin told him.

'Wait a minute,' Jacob interrupted. 'You said we. Was there someone else with you?'

Calvin nodded. 'A boy named Ajay,' he said. 'It was his idea to run away in the first place. He believed that if you could find your way to the Palace of Remembrance, the king and queen would give you back everything you'd lost.'

'Everything you'd lost?' Jacob said. 'What does that mean?'

Calvin shrugged. 'Your memories, who knows, maybe even the life you left behind. That was what Ajay believed anyway.'

Jacob felt a shiver of excitement run through his body. 'Why did he think that?' he asked.

'It's part of the story,' Calvin told him, 'and Ajay believed every word of it.'

'Did you believe it?' Jacob asked.

Calvin was silent for a while. Finally, in a tone that sounded less certain, he said, 'It was worth a try.'

'But you didn't discover the Palace of Remembrance?'

'All we discovered was dirt and rocks,' Calvin said. 'That's all there is out there – dirt and rocks. Nothing else.'

'So you came back.'

'You got it.'

'I told you there was no story,' Stefan told Jacob. He stood up. 'Thanks for talking to us, Calvin,' he said.

'Any time,' Calvin said. 'See you around, Stefan.' He closed his eyes and began once again humming tunelessly to himself. The interview was clearly over.

Jacob also stood up. He was about to leave when a thought occurred to him. 'Where can I get hold of Ajay?' he asked.

Calvin's eyes opened again. 'You can't,' he said.

'Why not?'

'Because he didn't come back.'

'He didn't come back?'

'That's right.'

'How come?'

'Because he was a fool,' Calvin said. 'He wouldn't give up even when it was obvious there wasn't any point in going on.'

'But what happened to him?'

'I don't know. I expect he died out there.'

Jacob couldn't accept this. 'He's dead already,' he said reasonably. 'We're all dead. How can you die more than once?'

Calvin said nothing. He seemed to be thinking about this. Then, after a long time, he stood up. 'Let me get this straight,' he said. 'You think we're all dead, do you?'

'I know we are,' Jacob assured him.

'And you don't believe we can die again. Is that it?'

'Yes.'

Quite suddenly and without any warning, Calvin leaned forward and slapped Jacob hard across the face. The shock made him stagger backwards. He put his hand up to his cheek which was stinging from the blow. 'What was that for?' he demanded.

'Did you feel it?' Calvin asked.

'Of course I felt it,' Jacob said indignantly. 'It hurt.'

Calvin nodded. 'You told me what you believed. Now I'm telling you what I believe. If you can hurt, you can die. Understand?'

Slowly Jacob nodded. Calvin's meaning was crystal clear: one death was not necessarily the end.

'You want to find Ajay?' Calvin went on. 'Go look for his bones. They're out there with the dirt and rocks.'

10. THE ROAD TO NOWHERE

In the days that followed Jacob could not get the Palace of Remembrance out of his thoughts. Its image loomed at the back of his mind, growing stronger and stronger, and he asked himself whether it could possibly be true. Even though Calvin had been scornful of the idea, he must once have believed in it strongly enough to set out on his journey. And what about Ajay? Were his bones really lying out there somewhere beyond the stone-picking fields? Or had he reached his destination?

He repeated to himself what Calvin had told him about the king and queen who lived there, that they could give you back everything you had lost, not just your memories but maybe even the life you had left behind. At last he made up his mind to go in search of the Palace of Remembrance himself, whatever the cost.

It wasn't an easy decision to make. He would be on his own again, faced with the same appalling sense of isolation he'd felt when he had first woken up in the field by the river. And although there was nothing about Locus that he was fond of, it was at least familiar. In a world without a past, that was something to cling to. To leave it would be to turn his back on his friends. There would be no one to cheer him up when his courage failed and no one but himself to blame if it all came to nothing. But it still seemed to him that he had no choice. He was like someone who had dwelt in complete darkness for a long time and suddenly glimpses a chink of light.

He had arranged to meet with Aysha on the next rest day to talk about what had happened at the séance. To his surprise, Toby asked if he could come along, too. After breakfast the two of them made their way through the narrow streets towards the little square with the wooden benches. There was no sign of Aysha when they got there but she arrived a few minutes later. She did not seem put out at seeing Toby, giving him the same grave smile that she bestowed on Jacob. There was no doubt about it, Jacob decided, she was not the same girl that he had first met. She had become altogether more serious, deeper somehow. She turned her keen, brown eyes on him. 'How have you been?' she asked.

'Up and down,' Jacob said.

She nodded as if she needed no further explanation.

'But I've got something important to tell you,' he went on. 'Both of you,' he added, for although Toby knew about his visit to Calvin, Jacob had remained tight-lipped about the details of their conversation, preferring to think things through first. Now he explained exactly what had happened, even describing how Calvin had slapped him at the end.

'Stefan always said he was weird,' Toby pointed out.

'I wouldn't say he was weird,' Jacob replied. 'I think he's very clever and brave, too. It must have taken a lot of courage to start out on that journey. But I also think he regrets coming back.'

'Did he say that?' Aysha asked.

'No he didn't. In fact he implied the opposite,' Jacob replied, 'and maybe I'm wrong. It's just a guess. But that's the feeling I got when I thought about it afterwards. I felt that deep down in himself he still believes in the Palace of Remembrance. That's why he doesn't like to talk about it very much.'

The other two thought about this. Then Aysha spoke. 'What about you?' she asked. 'Do you believe in it?'

'I don't know,' Jacob said. 'When you first told me that you thought we were dead I didn't believe it but now I do. So I'm not sure it's really possible for me to say. It doesn't matter anyway, because I've made up my mind that I'm going to look for it and, whatever happens, I'm not coming back. That was what I wanted to tell you.' As he said this he felt the burden of loneliness once more begin to descend upon him. While his decision had remained unspoken, it had always been possible to change his mind. Now he had committed himself and he realised that he was not just telling his friends about his decision, he was saying goodbye to them.

'But the whole thing may just be a dream,' Toby said.

'I realise that,' Jacob told him. 'But isn't it better to go in search of a dream than to spend your time picking up stones in a land without hope?'

Toby nodded slowly. 'Maybe you're right,' he said. 'When were you thinking of leaving?'

'As soon as possible,' Jacob replied.

Aysha had remained silent since asking Jacob whether

or not he believed in the story of the palace. Now she spoke. 'I'm coming with you,' she said, calmly and quietly but with a voice full of determination.

Immediately Jacob felt a huge sense of relief. He would not be alone after all. Nevertheless, he felt he ought to try and dissuade her. 'You don't have to do that,' he said.

'I know,' she replied. 'But I want to come. You're right about this place. We can't stay here. We're not really living at all. We're just killing time and I don't want to do that any more.'

'I'm coming, too,' Toby said.

They both looked at him. His face showed none of the certainty of Aysha's and Jacob could have sworn that his voice had trembled slightly. 'Maybe you should think about it first,' he suggested.

'If I think about it too much, I won't do it,' Toby said. 'You have to let me come.'

'Of course you can come,' Jacob said. He found himself smiling for the first time in ages.

They decided to set off on the following rest day when there would be no one working in the stone-picking fields. 'We should leave early in the morning,' Aysha said, 'as soon as it gets light. That way we stand a chance of being well away before there's anyone around.'

'Do you think they'll make any attempt to stop us?' Toby asked nervously.

'I'm not sure,' Jacob replied, 'but somehow I doubt it. I mean the supervision here is very lax, isn't it?'

'Maybe that's because there's nowhere to go,' Toby suggested.

It was obvious that Toby's resolution was not very strong. He could become downcast and dispirited very quickly. It occurred to Jacob that this might prove a problem in the days ahead. 'Maybe there isn't anywhere to go,' he replied. 'Maybe we're taking a road to nowhere. But it's the only road I can see and it leads out of here. That's good enough for me.'

There weren't many arrangements to make. They agreed that they would each take an extra lunch box from the dining hall on the two days before they left, so they would have food and drink for the journey. And they decided it might be best if they did not go to bed the night before. That was the only way they could be sure to wake early enough. 'We can always find somewhere to sleep once we're past the stone-picking fields,' said Aysha.

It was hard to resist the temptation to tell the others about their plans but they had agreed that secrecy was best. The night before they left, the truth would have to come out, of course, because Aysha would be spending the night in their dormitory. Until then, however, they would keep the whole affair to themselves. But there was something about their manner over the next few days, a subdued excitement perhaps, that made some of the other boys glance oddly at Toby and Jacob. It was Stefan who finally questioned them.

'What are you two up to?' he asked one morning as they sat in the dining hall eating their breakfast.

'Who, us?' Toby asked trying to sound as innocent as possible but looking distinctly guilty.

'We're just enjoying the delights of another meal in Locus,' Jacob told him.

Stefan nodded as if Jacob's answer confirmed what he'd already been thinking. 'You're never going to give up, are you?' he asked.

Jacob looked at him uncertainly. A sense of unease began gnawing at him as he wondered how much Stefan had guessed.

But Stefan must have known what he was thinking because he gave a wry smile. 'Don't worry about me,' he said. 'I can keep a secret.'

In any case, he didn't have to keep it for long. At last there was only one day to wait. His final day in Locus, Jacob told himself. That evening, after dinner, Aysha came back to their dormitory. The others were surprised to see her. 'Are we h-h-holding another séance?' Ivor wanted to know.

Jacob shook his head. 'Toby, Aysha and I are leaving very early tomorrow morning,' he said. 'We're not coming back.'

'I suppose you're going to look for the Palace of Remembrance,' Stefan said.

'Yes, we are,' Jacob replied. He waited for Stefan to utter some scathing remark, but Stefan remained silent. Then after a little while he said, 'Well I wish you luck.'

At first Jacob was too surprised to reply. Then, pulling himself together, he said, 'Thanks, Stefan.'

It was harder than they had imagined to stay awake once the lights had gone out. At first they sat in the darkness listening to the others playing the memory game.

Then, as the voices became increasingly sleepy and finally died away altogether, they whispered together about their own memories. But soon they had run out of things to say to each other and there was nothing left to do but sit and wait for the night to pass. At last, after he had found himself drifting off to sleep for the third time, Jacob came to a decision. 'Let's not wait for dawn,' he said. 'Let's leave now. Otherwise we're going to fall asleep and miss our chance.' The others agreed. They got up, carrying a lunch box in each hand, crept quietly between the rows of sleeping boys, opened the front door and stepped out into the night.

The sky was a blaze of stars and they stood for a moment gazing up at it. Jacob had come to believe that nothing about Locus could be beautiful. But the night sky almost took his breath away. It was Aysha who called them back to the task in hand. 'Come on,' she said. 'We mustn't hang around here.'

They were not prepared for how cold it was outside. The thin fabric of their uniforms was not designed for night-time and within a few minutes they were all shivering. 'Let's run,' Jacob suggested. 'It will warm us up.' The others agreed and they set off at a jog, following the route that the bus took towards the stone-picking fields.

After they had warmed up, they settled down to walking briskly, every now and again breaking into a run when the cold got too much for them. Even travelling like this, it still took a long time to reach the start of the stone-picking fields. 'I wonder how far these go on,' Jacob said, as they made their way along the moonlit road.

'Quite a long way, I think,' Toby told him.

He was right. The roped-off areas seemed to continue for ever and the first traces of dawn were leaking into the sky before they finally left them behind. Once past the stone-picking fields, however, the road seemed to peter out altogether. They halted to consider their position. 'What do we do now?' Toby asked.

'Just keep going, I suppose,' Jacob said. 'I think the sun sets in that direction,' he added, pointing ahead and to their right.

It was hard to tell much about the countryside in which they now found themselves because it was still quite dark. But what light there was showed a barren plain. Here and there a few stunted trees broke the monotony but essentially it was just as Calvin had described it: nothing but dirt and rocks.

'We might as well press on,' Jacob said.

'We could look for somewhere to get some sleep,' Aysha suggested.

'Good idea,' Jacob agreed.

But finding somewhere to rest in this arid landscape was not easy. They continued walking as the world brightened around them while they began to feel dreadfully weary. At last Toby said, 'We'll have to stop soon. I'm nearly walking in my sleep.' They sat down beside a couple of stunted-looking trees which didn't offer much shelter but were better than nothing. They opened their lunch boxes, ate and drank a little, then lay down on the ground and slept.

*

It was the middle of the day and the sun felt hot on his head as Jacob crouched on the top of the wire fence, trying to get his balance before leaping down. The fence was not built to take his weight and it wobbled slightly so that he half-jumped, half-fell, landing on his hands and knees on the other side. He wasn't hurt, but he grabbed hold of a nettle as he landed so his hand was tingling where he had been stung. He got to his feet, rubbing his hand against his thigh, conscious that he was late and that the others would be waiting for him. He made his way through dense undergrowth, down a slope along a rough path. As he pushed his way through a clump of brambles, he caught sight of them, looking impatiently in his direction. For some reason, now that he had found them, Jacob was reluctant to go down and meet them. He had run all the way here, and scrambled precariously over the fence. But now he was not sure that he wanted to go any further. One of them, a tall youth with cropped hair and a sneer on his face, called out to him, 'Are you coming down here or what?'

Without bothering to reply Jacob went down to join them.

The boy with the cropped hair began talking. He had a harsh, unfriendly voice and Jacob could not help noticing that he spat slightly as he pronounced certain words. He was telling the others what was expected of them. But Jacob was not listening to his words. He kept looking at the boy's face, at the way his lips curled when he spoke, and the tiny droplets of spit that were projected from his mouth. Suddenly the boy stopped. He must have noticed that Jacob was staring at him oddly. 'What's up with you, weirdo?' he demanded.

Jacob knew he was being insulted but for some reason he did not really care. He glanced wistfully back along the way he had come. He could just make out the wire fence over the tops of the bushes and he noticed a bird perched where only a moment ago he had crouched, trying to get his balance before jumping to the ground. As he watched, the bird turned its head and Jacob felt for a moment that it was looking directly at him. Then it opened its beak and began to sing.

He woke and sat up, uncertain at first where he was. Then he remembered. Toby and Aysha were still asleep. Toby's mouth was open and he was making little snuffling noises like some sort of animal. Jacob stood up and wandered a little way from the trees, in order to stretch his legs. It had been the same dream and, once again, he felt convinced it had been telling him something but no matter how hard he tried he could not understand what that was. The more he struggled to puzzle it out, the more the details of the dream retreated until only tattered images remained like torn rags caught on a bush, fluttering in the wind before blowing away completely.

11. THE DEDANIM

Toby and Aysha woke up shortly afterwards and the three of them set off again. The excitement they had felt on first stepping out of the dormitory under a starry sky disappeared completely as they grew accustomed to plodding relentlessly over miles and miles of dusty ground. After a while, Toby said, 'The others will probably be having breakfast by now.'

Jacob nodded. It was hard to tell how much of the morning had passed. The clear blue sky of daybreak had given way to a mass of grey cloud which hid the sun from view. But he guessed that Toby was right. They were out of sight of even the most far-flung of the stone-picking fields by now and, unless search parties were sent out to look for them, it seemed as if the first part of their plan had been successful. Now all they had to do was find the Palace of Remembrance.

Around the middle of the day they rested and ate what was left of the food in the first set of lunch boxes. It might have been wiser to save some for supper but the portions were not particularly big and once they began to eat it was impossible to stop until the food was finished. Before they set off again they dug a hole and buried the empty lunch boxes, taking only the bottles of drink with them.

When he had been making his plans, Jacob had not expected walking all day to be so exhausting. The temptation to stop and lie down became harder and harder to resist and by evening they were all desperately tired. When they finally called a halt, in the shelter of huge boulders that looked as if they had been dropped there carelessly by some ancient race of giants, Toby took off his shoes and socks and showed them where the blisters on his feet had burst and the skin beneath was broken and bleeding. But Jacob and Aysha were too busy feeling sorry for themselves to waste much pity on him. Now they bitterly regretted eating all of their ration in the middle of the day.

'Maybe we should just have a little bit of tomorrow's food,' Toby suggested.

'I don't think that's a good idea,' Jacob said. 'We'll need it even more tomorrow. We've got to be disciplined.'

Toby looked at Aysha. 'I agree with Jacob,' she told him. 'Remember, we'll have nothing at all for the third day.'

'We should have brought more food with us,' Toby complained.

'Yes, but we didn't,' Jacob said.

'How could we have been so stupid?' Toby went on.

'Stop whining, Toby,' Aysha said.

The sharpness of her tone took Toby by surprise. He looked at her as if she had slapped him and for a moment Jacob thought he might burst into tears. But then he pulled himself together. 'Sorry,' he said.

'The best thing to do is to try to get as much sleep as possible,' Jacob declared.

The other two nodded. The three of them stretched out on the ground and closed their eyes. Despite the discomfort of their situation, they were asleep within moments.

In the middle of the night Jacob awoke. It was the sound of some animal howling in the distance that had dragged him from sleep. That and the cold. Shivering, he wrapped his arms around himself.

'Are you awake?' Aysha whispered.

'Yes.'

'I'm freezing,' she said.

'Me too. Do you think we should get up and start walking again?'

'No. We won't be able to tell which direction we're going in. Let's put our arms around each other instead,' she said.

Jacob moved closer to her and they wrapped their arms around each other. He could feel her breath on his cheek and her hair tickling his forehead. 'I'm glad you came,' he told her.

'So am I,' she said.

'Are you really? Even though it's so hard.'

'Yes, I am,' she said.

Then they went back to sleep, neither of them waking again until morning.

It was a wail that woke Jacob this time, the sound of another human being in distress. He sat up and looked around in confusion. Not very far away, he could see Toby staring into an open lunch box and it was clear that the sound had come from him.

'What's the matter?' Jacob asked.

Toby turned and looked at him. On his face was an expression of complete misery. 'The food!' he said.

'What about it?'

'Look at it!' He handed the lunch box to Jacob who looked inside. Instead of the spongy white food there was just a little pile of dust. 'What happened to it?' Jacob asked.

Toby shrugged. 'It's shrivelled up or something,' he said. 'The others are exactly the same. That must be what happens if you try to keep it for too long. We should have eaten it last night!'

Jacob felt stung by this. After all, it was he who had insisted on saving the food until today and he felt that Toby was blaming him for what had occurred. 'We didn't know this would happen,' he said grudgingly.

'What's going on?' asked Aysha, who had been woken by the commotion.

Jacob explained what had happened and she listened without interrupting. When he had finished she simply said, 'There's no point in making a fuss about it. We'll just have to carry on as we are.'

Jacob felt grateful to her for not allocating blame.

Fortunately the same thing had not happened to the drink and they allowed themselves just a little before setting off again. It was hard not to dwell on what had happened and for the first part of the morning none of them said very much. Jacob still felt that Toby considered him responsible and this irritated him. It was Toby who finally broke the silence.

'I had a new memory yesterday,' he said.

'Tell us about it,' Aysha suggested.

'I remembered being on holiday with my parents.'

The word 'holiday' had been quite unknown to Jacob before now but as Toby spoke it seemed to uncurl in his mind, growing into meaning like a flower opening towards the sun. He remembered that a holiday was a time when you stopped your normal life and did something different, like visiting a faraway place. It was a time of great excitement and he felt some of that excitement steal over him now.

'We were in a car,' Toby continued. 'My father was driving and I remember looking out of the window at a sign by the roadside.'

'What did it say?' Jacob asked.

'I don't know,' Toby told him. 'I couldn't understand it.'

'Why not?'

'Because it was in another language.'

'Another language,' Jacob repeated. This, too, began to have meaning for him. Of course! There were people who spoke languages other than his own. Those languages were just as good as his, they could be used to mean all the same things, but they were made up of entirely different words.

'What else happened?' Aysha asked.

'That's all I remember,' Toby said. 'But afterwards, I couldn't help wondering: where are all the people who've died, like us, but who speak other languages? I mean everyone in Locus seems to speak the same language. So where are the others?'

'Does it matter?' Jacob asked.

'I think it does,' Toby said.

'Well maybe they're all in a different part of Locus,' Jacob suggested. 'We don't know how big it is, remember. Or maybe everyone speaks the same language once they're dead.'

'My father spoke a different language,' Aysha said, suddenly. 'Not all the time, just sometimes. I've only just remembered that.'

'Another thing that struck me was this,' Toby went on. 'Everyone in Locus is more or less the same age as us.'

'Except for the adults,' Jacob pointed out.

'Yes but there aren't very many of them, are there?' Toby replied. 'So what happens to all the people who die at different ages: babies or old people, for example. Where are they?'

'Who knows?' Jacob said. He still couldn't see why this was important.

'Yes but there should be at least as many adults as there are children,' Toby went on. 'More probably. But we only see Virgil and Berith and the bus driver and they seem to belong there.'

'What about the minions?' Jacob replied. 'We don't know how many of them there are.'

'I don't think they were ever alive,' Toby said. 'Not like we were, anyway. They're only half-alive now, if you ask me. They just exist to keep the place going.'

'You know what I think?' Aysha asked.

'What?'

'I think that maybe there isn't just one place where

people go when they die. I think there might be any number of different places. Hundreds, maybe millions, I don't know.'

'So how come we've all ended up together?' Toby asked.

'Perhaps it just worked out like that,' Jacob replied.

'Or maybe there's a reason,' Aysha said.

'What sort of reason?'

'Maybe we've got something to learn from each other.'

'Yes,' Toby said, excitedly. 'That's what I thought. I mean, I've been thinking all morning that I wouldn't have run away on my own. I needed other people to egg me on. And then, when I found we'd got no food left, I felt like turning back.'

Jacob was dismayed. He had felt miserable about the food but the idea of turning back had never even occurred to him. At the same time he felt it was important that Toby should not feel he had to stay with them. 'You can turn back if you want to,' he assured him.

Toby shook his head. 'I don't want to,' he said. 'That's the point. I want to keep going but on my own I'm not sure I could do it. That's why I need you two.'

There was something very innocent-looking about his expression when he said this and Jacob could imagine what he must have looked like as a very young child. He found himself forgiving Toby's complaints about not eating the food the previous night. It was just that Toby was not as strong as he was, or as Aysha for that matter. But Toby had other qualities. He was warm-hearted and there was something about him that seemed to make the other two feel stronger. 'We need you too, Toby,' Jacob said.

By the time they halted in the middle of the day, Jacob's legs were trembling with weakness and he thought they might give way at any moment. The three of them lay down beside a withered stump of a tree, grateful at last to have stopped the endless march across rocky ground. They allowed themselves a few precious sips of their drinks. No one said anything further about the lack of food but inwardly they all bemoaned the folly of setting off from Locus with such scanty supplies. For the last few hours Jacob had been wondering vaguely whether they might discover anything to eat in their environment, but the whole landscape was barren. As he reluctantly put the top back on his bottle of drink, he thought again of Calvin's words, and of the fate that he believed his friend Ajay had suffered. Was the same thing going to happen to them?

He closed his eyes. It was not his intention to go to sleep, merely to rest for a little while but he was immediately aware, when he opened them again, that a considerable amount of time had passed. Though the sun was hidden behind a thick layer of clouds, it was still possible to tell that its position in the sky had changed. Jacob guessed it must be late afternoon by now. He turned to call the others who were lying asleep beside him but before he could do so, his attention was caught by something moving in the distance. He stood up to see more clearly and strained his eyes towards the horizon. It looked like a dust cloud but it seemed to be getting larger all the time. Dismayed, he wondered whether it might be some peculiar sort of storm but suddenly realised what it was: people on horseback.

'Aysha! Toby!' he shouted.

The other two sat up and looked blearily about them. 'What is it?' Aysha asked.

'Riders,' Jacob told them. 'Coming towards us.'

Aysha and Toby scrambled to their feet and gazed in the direction he was pointing. There could be no mistake. A band of riders was moving in their direction, travelling at considerable speed.

'Do you think they've been sent to look for us?' Toby asked.

'They're coming from the other direction to Locus,' Jacob pointed out.

'Maybe we should hide all the same,' Toby suggested.

'Where?' Aysha asked.

They looked all around. There was absolutely nowhere to hide. 'We'll just have to wait and see what they have to say for themselves,' Jacob said.

The first thing that became clear as the riders drew nearer was that they did not wear the familiar grey uniforms of Locus. On the contrary, their clothes seemed to be made up of every colour under the sun, each garment a patchwork of hues, as if it was their wish to draw as much attention to themselves as possible. Men and women rode together side by side, both sexes dressed in baggy breeches and short-sleeved tunics. The women wore their hair long, tied back with bands of silver and gold that flashed as they rode. The men were bearded but their hair was cropped. Their arms and their necks were covered in tattoos.

As they drew within hailing distance, the man at the

head of the column raised his hand, and all the riders suddenly came to a halt. Then the leader spoke in a loud, clear voice. 'Greetings, my friends.'

'Greetings,' Jacob replied, uncertainly.

'May I ask what brings you to these parts?' the man continued.

Jacob hesitated, unsure how much it was wise to tell this stranger. But before he could make up his mind, Toby spoke. 'We're looking for the Palace of Remembrance,' he said.

Immediately there was an outbreak of laughter from the riders. The man who had spoken raised his hand and the laughter died away again as quickly as it had begun. 'Then I fear you are wasting your time,' he said gravely, 'for there is no such place.'

'Are you sure?' Toby demanded.

'Quite sure,' the man replied. 'The Palace of Remembrance is a story, no more.'

'But how can you be certain of that?' Aysha demanded. 'Maybe you just haven't come across it.'

The man smiled at her sadly. 'You do not understand to whom you speak,' he told her. 'We are the travelling Dedanim. This land is our home and we are familiar with every bush and every rock. If there were truly such a palace, do you think we would not know of it?'

He spoke with such conviction that it was impossible to doubt his words. Jacob turned to see how the others had taken the news. Toby was staring straight ahead of him, like someone who had been turned to stone. Aysha had covered her face with her hands.

The leader of the Dedanim was looking at her with dismay. Now he spoke again. 'Do not cry, little girl,' he said.

His words seemed to galvanise Aysha. She took her hands away from her face and her eyes blazed angrily back at him. 'I'm not crying,' she said defiantly, 'and I'm not a little girl, either.'

Jacob was alarmed, feeling sure that her words would make the man angry but he only nodded his head, as if he understood perfectly how she felt. 'I beg your pardon, young lady,' he said. 'It was not my intention to mock you. Perhaps I can make amends by asking you and your companions to share a meal with us.'

Aysha glanced at the other two and saw, from their reactions, that they found this suggestion as welcome as she did herself. 'Thank you very much,' she said. 'We'd love to.'

The speed with which the Dedanim dismounted and set up camp was remarkable. Soon they had a fire blazing and round about it they spread rugs as colourful as their clothes. They began to cook, the men and the women working together. As they worked, they joked and laughed so that Jacob, Toby and Aysha felt cheered just by watching them. Soon they were even more heartened by the smell of the food being prepared. Their mouths watered and their stomachs rumbled until at last the food was served on silver platters.

Jacob could not have put a name to anything that appeared on the plate in front of him but he felt certain that for the first time since they had arrived in Locus, he was being offered real food. Eagerly, he put some in his mouth and found that the taste was even more wonderful than the smell. He looked at the others and it was clear from their faces that they shared his pleasure.

As they ate, the Dedanim leader asked them questions about their journey. He knew about Locus. The grey town, he called it. 'We do not go there,' he said. 'The very thought of it fills us with sadness.'

'So where do you live?' Jacob asked.

The Dedanim leader spread his hands wide. 'As I told you,' he said, 'we are the wandering Dedanim. We live beneath the sky, spending a few days here and a few days there. We are not tied to one place, like a horse tethered to a post.'

He grinned as he said this and it seemed to Jacob that the life of the Dedanim was an enviable one.

When they had eaten and drunk so much that their stomachs felt stretched, the Dedanim leader looked up at the sky. 'It is time for us to move on,' he said. 'This is not a good place to spend the night.'

'Where will you spend the night?' Aysha asked.

'Many miles from here,' the Dedanim leader told her. 'We know a place where there is flowing water and trees that offer shelter.'

His description filled them with a sense of longing. As if he realised this, he paused for a moment. Then he said, 'Why not come with us? We have spare horses. Unless, of course, you would rather continue your search for the Palace of Remembrance.'

'We'd love to come with you,' Toby said enthusiastically. Then he turned and looked uncertainly at the others. 'Wouldn't we?' he asked.

Jacob looked at Aysha. She said nothing but he could tell from her expression that she wanted to agree. For a moment his mind dwelled on the Palace of Remembrance, the promise at the heart of the story that the king and queen could give you back all you had lost. Then he pushed the thought away. It was a story for children. He addressed the leader of the Dedanim. 'We'd be honoured to come with you,' he said.

The Dedanim leader stood up. 'Our guests have agreed to join us,' he shouted. A great cheer sprang up from his followers.

12. A VOICE IN THE WIND

Riding with the Dedanim was like being a part of some great, happy, extended family. One man, with a thick black beard, showed Jacob how to sit on his horse and how to hold the reins. Another, whose teeth glinted with gold, rode beside him and called out a series of well-meaning comments. Others made jokes and sang songs. Jacob could not remember the names of any of them but it did not matter. They still turned to him with their bright eyes and flashing smiles, amused by his attempts to control the horse but too polite to laugh out loud. It was the same for Aysha and Toby. They sat aloft the spirited animals the Dedanim had found for them, concentrating furiously on trying to stay in the saddle, looking up from time to time to see faces smiling encouragingly at them. Fortunately, the horses seemed to know what they were doing at least as well as their riders, and the Dedanim did not travel at speed. Soon Jacob, Toby and Aysha found a rhythm into which they could settle while the miles of rocky ground passed by beneath their horses' hooves.

In time, the scenery around them began to change. There were trees and bushes; grass grew beneath their feet. Even the air smelled different: moist, earthy, filled with the scent of growing things. At last the Dedanim leader raised his hand and once more the column came to a halt. Now that the sound of cantering hooves had ceased, Jacob was aware of another noise. He was uncertain what it was at first but then some buried part of his memory resurfaced and identified it: it was the sound of swiftly running water.

The Dedanim all dismounted. Jacob, Toby and Aysha followed suit. Their horses were led away to where there was plenty of grass for grazing. After so long in the saddle, Jacob's legs felt wobbly beneath him and he walked back and forth to accustom himself to being on his own two feet again while all around him the Dedanim were busy erecting their camp, building a fire, preparing a meal. He found his way to the water. It was no more than a small stream flowing down from some distant hills but it seemed immensely beautiful to him. He bent down and splashed some water on his face. It felt deliciously cool.

'Looks like things haven't turned out so badly after all,' Toby said, joining him beside the stream. 'We may not have found the Palace of Remembrance but this is certainly better than Locus. At least the Dedanim seem to enjoy life.' He bent down, cupped some of the water in his hands and drank.

Jacob nodded. He did not find it as easy as Toby to forget his dream of regaining all that he had lost, but he could not deny that the company in which they now found themselves was altogether more agreeable than their dreary existence in Locus.

Just then Aysha appeared beside them wearing a

112

beaming smile on her face. 'I've just been talking to Letushim,' she told them.

'To who?'

'Letushim. That's the leader's name. I said it must be great to be so free, to be able to travel wherever you like and do what you like. I said I envied him and do you know what he said?'

'What?'

'He said, there is no need for envy, young lady. You and your companions are most welcome to make your home among the Dedanim.'

Toby's face lit up with delight at these words. 'We've really fallen on our feet, haven't we?' he said.

Jacob nodded. 'Yes, we have,' he replied, but he spoke without Toby's enthusiasm.

'What's the matter?' Aysha asked him.

'Nothing,' Jacob told her. 'It's just that . . .'

'Just that what?'

'Oh I don't know. I suppose I just find it difficult to let go of my hope that I could one day, somehow get back, you know.'

Aysha nodded slowly. She reached out and took his hands in hers. 'Poor Jacob,' she said.

'I'm all right,' Jacob told her. 'I'm just being silly.' He withdrew his hands from Aysha's. 'It's a wonderful, generous offer and I should be enormously grateful,' he said. 'No. I am enormously grateful. In fact I'm so grateful that I'm going to see if I can do anything to help. After all, if we're going to join the Dedanim, we can't keep on behaving like guests, can we?'

Jacob was not sure whether the Dedanim really did need any help but they allowed him, Aysha and Toby to join in with their preparations, showing them how the food was cooked and laughing when Jacob asked what it was.

'This is meat,' a man called Asshurim told him.

'Where does it come from?' Toby asked.

Again there was a great deal of laughter. 'This land is full of animals,' Asshurim replied, 'but most of the time they remain hidden. The time to catch them is just before dawn. That is when we hunt. Come with us in the hour before daybreak and you will see where we get our meat.'

There were many other things the Dedanim used in their cooking: roots dug out of the ground, the leaves and fruits of plants. As Jacob listened to them describing the origins of all these ingredients, he felt surprise give way to familiarity. Yes, he felt sure that cooking must have been like that in the life he had left behind.

The results were certainly worth all the effort and as Jacob sat around the fire with the others, finishing off the sweet dish that had completed the meal, he recalled the misgivings he had briefly entertained about joining the Dedanim. 'How could I have been so stupid?' he asked himself. He put his empty plate on the rug in front of him and smiled a long, satisfied smile. Toby was right. They had certainly fallen on their feet.

The Dedanim slept out in the open but they covered themselves with blankets and there were plenty of these to go round. Jacob took his bundle gratefully, reflecting on the fact that at least tonight he would be able to enjoy an uninterrupted night's sleep. He made his bed under the trees, shut his eyes and waited for sleep to overtake him.

To his surprise, however, sleep proved elusive. Although he was extremely tired and his body ached from a morning walking across stony ground and an afternoon learning to ride, he found himself unable to relax and surrender to the emptiness of sleep. After a while he gave up trying altogether and lay awake looking up at the starry sky and listening to the sounds of the Dedanim camp: the crackle of the fire, the soft murmur of those who remained awake and the occasional whinnying of the horses.

The wind began to get up and ragged wisps of cloud were driven across the face of the moon. The trees around Jacob sighed and creaked as gusts battered their branches. The sound was new to him, and yet familiar too, like so many things that called up buried memories. He wondered if he had lain awake out in the open like this in his former life, listening to the sighing of the wind in the trees. These thoughts saddened him and the excitement that he had felt earlier in the evening about joining the Dedanim died away. He remembered how he had lain awake in his dormitory in Locus and sworn to himself that he would find a way back to the life that had been taken from him. These were pointless thoughts, he told himself. That life was gone and there was no hope of recovering it. But he could do nothing about the waves of sadness that swept over him, carried on the night wind.

Everyone else had settled down to sleep by now; even the horses were quiet, and he felt as if he were the only person left awake in the entire world. He turned restlessly from side to side, then onto his back once more. But it was no good. Sleep seemed as far away as ever. He opened his eyes again and gazed up at the sky. He wondered if all the stars had names. Directly above him there was one star that seemed brighter than all the others. And for some reason Jacob felt himself drawn to it. He found that as he looked at it, it seemed to change in shape, twinkling and growing brighter, like a candle burning in the sky. Fascinated, he stared fixedly now, focusing his whole attention upon this single point of light, and as he did so he began to feel as if he was floating upwards towards it or as if it was floating downwards towards him. At the same time the point of light grew larger until it was like a tunnel that he was gliding along, a tunnel that stretched on and on until suddenly it came to an end and he felt himself tumbling into somewhere utterly familiar yet also somehow shocking. Where was he? Of course. He was in the living room of his house again and there sitting at the table was his mother, with tears in her eyes.

'Jacob,' she said.

'Mum,' he replied.

'Why don't you answer me, Jacob?' she went. 'If you are still around, in some way. If your spirit is still here, then why don't you give me some sort of sign?'

'I'm here, Mum,' he told her. 'I'm in the room with you right now.'

'You know I really felt that you were around,' she continued, 'that you hadn't completely gone, that you were still in touch somehow. But now that feeling has gone. I can't even see your face in my mind. Why is that? Why can't I see your face any more? I don't want to forget you, Jacob.' She began to sob out loud.

Jacob crossed the room until he was standing right beside her. 'Please don't cry, Mum,' he told her. He reached out his hand to touch her but there was nothing there to touch. His hand went right through her arm and he felt as if he had plunged it into ice-cold water. The shock made him recoil backwards and at the same time it seemed that the ground was moving beneath his feet. It was a sickening feeling and he struggled to keep his balance as the room began to turn around him, gently at first like a leaf in a breeze but then faster and faster until it was nothing but a dizzying blur. He opened his eyes to discover that he was lying beneath the stars in the camp of the Dedanim.

What did it mean, he wondered? From somewhere deep within himself came the answer. He had been wrong to give up his search for the Palace of Remembrance. That was why his mother was losing her memory of him, that was why she could no longer see his face in her mind. It was because he had given up the belief that he could return. No, he had not really given it up; it had been taken from him. The Dedanim had stolen it with their laughter and their insistence that the Palace of Remembrance was no more than a story. They had defeated him far more easily than Virgil or Berith or the stultifying routines of Locus. They had charmed his belief away from him.

Not any longer. Tomorrow, he would politely decline their company, he would turn his back on them and return the way he had come. But even as he made this resolution, he thought how terribly hard it would be to retrace on foot the many miles that had been covered on horseback. And yet it had to be done. Now that he had made this decision, he fell easily and quickly into a dreamless sleep.

As soon as he woke the next morning he remembered his experience during the night and the conclusion he had come to. It still felt right. Heartened by this conviction, but at the same time intimidated at the thought of putting it into practice, he sat up and looked around him. The camp was in motion. The Dedanim were busy washing clothes, grooming horses, and preparing food. He looked for Aysha and Toby and found them yawning, stretching and looking around with expressions of bleary-eyed contentment. He could tell immediately that they would not want to hear his news. Nevertheless, there was nothing else to be done. He began to explain what had happened to him.

Toby looked sceptical. 'It sounds to me as if you just had a dream,' he said. 'You were probably thinking about our decision to join the Dedanim, and I expect you were still upset about the Palace of Remembrance turning out to be nothing but a story. So when you went to sleep it all got mixed up in your mind.'

Jacob shook his head. 'It wasn't a dream,' he said.

'But Jacob,' Aysha objected, 'even if it is true, how could you possibly go all the way back again on foot?'

'I don't know,' Jacob replied. 'I only know it's what I have to do.'

'You'll starve,' Toby said. 'This is crazy!'

'I'm not asking either of you to come with me,' Jacob told them. He found it hard to say this because in his heart he dreaded the idea of making the journey by himself.

Indeed the loneliness seemed a worse prospect than the miles and miles of walking.

As the three of them stood in silence, Letushim came over and joined them. 'You are looking very grave, my friends,' he said. 'Is something troubling you?'

'I've decided I cannot join you, after all,' Jacob told him. 'I know this sounds very ungrateful and I'm sorry, but I have to go back and carry on searching for the Palace of Remembrance.'

Letushim shook his head in disbelief. 'This is nonsense,' he told Jacob. 'Your mind is still clouded with sleep. Did you not hear what I said yesterday? There is no such palace. It is only a story.'

'I know,' Jacob replied, 'and I realise that my decision must seem like madness to you but it's what I have to do.'

'Your decision does not merely seem like madness; it is madness,' Letushim said grimly. 'You must forget this.'

Jacob shook his head. 'I can't forget it,' he said. 'But I want you to know that I'm really grateful to you and to the rest of the Dedanim for the hospitality you have shown me. It's been the—'

'Enough!' Letushim interrupted angrily. 'I will not hear this foolishness. You are Dedanim now. When we have eaten, you will ride with us. There will be no argument.'

The fury with which he spoke took Jacob completely by surprise. It was as if he had become an entirely different person from the polite and gracious man whom they had met the previous day. Someone much more frightening now stood before them, hands on hips and eyes glittering with subdued rage. But his outburst only made Jacob even more certain that his decision to leave the Dedanim had been the right one. The sooner he was away from here, the better. He made up his mind to remain calm. 'I'm sorry,' he said, struggling to keep his voice from trembling, 'but I just can't do that. I'm really grateful to you for everything you've done for me but I'm afraid I do have to leave and I think it's probably best if I go now.'

'You will not go anywhere!' Letushim shouted. His right hand grasped the hilt of his sword.

He was a big man and Jacob guessed that he was enormously strong. He had no doubt that Letushim could kill him if he so wished and that the sensible thing to do would be to agree to whatever he demanded. But another part of him simply refused to be told what to do. Summoning all of his courage, he forced himself to speak. 'You're wrong,' he said. 'I'm leaving and you can't stop me.'

Letushim's manner suddenly changed. It seemed to Jacob that a sly look came over his face. 'You will not help your mother and father like this,' he said.

Jacob was startled. He had said nothing to Letushim about his parents. 'Who told you about them?' he demanded.

Letushim shrugged. 'You did.'

'No, I didn't.'

'You must have forgotten. It doesn't matter. It is still true. You will not keep them together by wandering off into the wilderness.'

But Jacob had stopped listening to him. Instead his mind was racing as he tried to make sense of what he had heard.

There was something very wrong about all this. 'I'm getting out of here,' he said. He took a step forward.

Letushim drew his sword. 'You will do as I tell you,' he said. He held the sword out in front of him and its edge gleamed in the morning sunlight.

Until that moment Jacob had been terrified but looking at Letushim standing there clutching his sword, he felt a strange calmness descend upon him. The man was a bully, nothing more, and Jacob was not going to be bullied. He shook his head. 'No, I won't,' he said quietly and firmly.

As he said this, something very peculiar began to happen. Letushim and everything around him seemed to ripple, as if it were a scene drawn upon cloth. There was a noise like a great rush of wind and then silence. Jacob looked around in bewilderment. Everything had changed. He was sitting on the ground beside the stump of a withered tree, just as he had been before he had first got to his feet and spied a cloud of dust coming towards him in the distance. There was no sign of the Dedanim.

13. NEMAIN

'I had the weirdest dream,' Aysha said, sitting up beside him and stretching. 'I dreamt we met these people on horseback who wanted us to join them.'

'So did I,' Toby said, wandering over towards them. 'They didn't want us to leave, either. The leader got very angry about it.'

'We all seem to have had the same dream,' Jacob mused. 'How very strange, if that's what it was.'

'Do you think it was real, then?' Aysha asked.

Jacob thought about it. 'The choice was real,' he said. 'But I think the Dedanim were just an illusion.'

'At least we haven't gone dozens of miles in the wrong direction,' Toby pointed out.

That much was true but it was little comfort beside the fact that there was nothing at all to eat and hardly anything to drink. Reluctantly, they brushed the dust off their clothes and set off walking again but their progress was very slow. Toby, in particular, seemed scarcely to have the strength to place one foot in front of the other. He was like a sleepwalker, hardly noticing when one of the other two spoke to him.

As the afternoon wore on, the landscape around them

began to change. The flat plain over which they had been walking in the morning gave way to hilly ground which slowed their progress considerably. After a while they stopped to rest under the shade of some trees. It seemed a long time since they had finished the drinks they had carried with them from Locus and it was hard now to think of anything other than how thirsty they were. They had been sitting in silence for a long time and Jacob had been wondering whether any of them really had the strength to start walking again when Aysha suddenly said, 'What's that noise?'

'I was wondering that,' Toby added.

'What noise?' Jacob asked. 'I can't hear anything.'

'Listen,' Toby told him.

Jacob listened carefully and found that there really was a noise, but it was so much part of the general background he had disregarded it until now. He tried as hard as he could to focus his hearing. The noise was like something moving but it did not seem to get any nearer or any further away. He was sure he had heard something like it very recently and suddenly he remembered where: it had been beside the Dedanim camp. 'It's a river!' he exclaimed.

'That's right!' Toby shouted and the three of them got to their feet.

'Which direction is it?' Jacob asked, excitedly.

They all listened carefully. Aysha turned slowly round in a circle. 'It's this way,' she said, setting off towards a thicket of enormous bushes with glossy green leaves.

The other two followed her, pushing their way through rubbery branches that whipped back at them and stung their faces and eyes. It was hard going but the sound was getting louder all the time. At last they were out of the bushes and there was the river in front of them. It was only a narrow channel running between rocky banks, nothing like the great stretch of water they had crossed with Virgil, but it was still a very welcome sight. They threw themselves on the ground, splashing their faces and laughing. Then they cupped the water in their hands and drank greedily. When they had finally slaked their thirst, they sat on the bank and dangled their feet in the water.

'You know this river runs more or less in the right direction for us,' Jacob observed, after a while.

'So we can just walk along the bank,' Toby suggested.

'I don't see why not.'

That was such a comforting thought. No longer would they be tormented by thirst. And at the back of Jacob's mind was the possibility that the river might lead them to the Palace of Remembrance. After all, whoever lived there must surely need water.

They were in much better humour when they set off again even though it was hard work following the line of the river. At first they had to make their way through more of the rubbery bushes that grew all along the bank but after a while these gave way to tall, thick grasses. At the same time, however, the ground became boggier and they frequently had to make wide detours to avoid flooded areas. The sun began to sink lower in the sky and the optimism they had felt when they first discovered the river began to ebb away. Now that their thirst had been satisfied, their thoughts turned to hunger. Jacob found himself craving the white, spongy food they had brought from Locus.

'Do you think we could eat any of the plants that grow around here?' Toby asked.

The other two looked doubtful. 'They might make us ill,' Aysha said.

'Eating nothing is going to make us even more ill,' Toby replied.

Jacob was about to agree with Aysha when he became aware of some sort of building up ahead. It was just visible through a stand of trees. He stopped and put his finger to his lips.

The other two looked at him anxiously and he pointed it out to them.

'Maybe it's the Palace of Remembrance,' Toby whispered.

'Maybe,' Jacob agreed. 'But it doesn't look very big and I somehow thought a palace would be a huge building.'

'So did I,' Aysha said. 'I think we should approach it very carefully.'

They crept forward, trying to make as little noise as possible. As they drew nearer, they could see that the building was very much smaller than the dormitories in Locus. It was built of irregular grey stones and the roof looked as if it had been made from bundles of the thick grass that grew all around. A pale column of smoke was drifting out of a chimney.

'If there's a fire, there must be someone inside,' Jacob said.

The other two nodded. 'What do we do?' Toby asked. 'Walk up to the front door and knock?'

'Let's wait a while,' Aysha suggested. 'Someone might come out.'

They lay in the long grass and waited while the sky above grew darker and evening approached. Jacob shivered as the temperature dropped. Nothing had happened for a long time and he was beginning to think that perhaps they should go and knock on the front door after all, when an old woman came out of the house carrying a bucket. She wore a long black dress and a black shawl over her head. They watched as she slowly made her way down to the river where she filled the bucket with water. Then she turned to go back to the house but it was clear that the bucket was almost too heavy for her and several times she was forced to stop and rest.

'She doesn't look very dangerous,' Jacob observed. 'I think we should go and ask her for help.'

'There might be someone else in the house,' Toby suggested.

'They wouldn't send her out for the water if there was,' Aysha objected. 'She can hardly carry it.'

'All right then,' Toby agreed.

The three of them walked towards the old woman. She didn't notice them until they were quite close. When she did, she was so startled that she spilled some of the water from her bucket.

'Hello,' Jacob called out.

The woman stared at him suspiciously.

'We haven't eaten all day,' he went on, 'and we're

exhausted. Could you possibly let us come into your house and rest and maybe give us something to eat?'

'Where have you come from?' the woman asked in a quavering voice.

'Locus,' Jacob told her.

She looked puzzled. 'The man with the clothes came only five days ago,' she said. 'I wasn't expecting anyone.'

Jacob wasn't sure what she was talking about. Did she think they had been sent from Locus on some sort of errand? He shook his head. 'We didn't come to check on you or anything,' he assured her.

'We were looking for the Palace of Remembrance and then we saw your house and we thought you might be able to help us,' Aysha added.

The woman frowned as if she found this difficult to understand. 'You haven't brought any clothes?' she asked.

'Only the ones we're wearing,' Toby told her.

Jacob could see her mouth moving as she repeated these words to herself, trying to make sense of them. 'If you give us some food, we can help you,' he said. 'I can carry the water for you.'

The woman thought about this for a moment. Then she nodded. 'Bring the bucket,' she said. She turned and began to walk towards the house.

Jacob picked up the bucket and they followed her into the house. It was simply furnished inside. A huge fireplace occupied most of one wall, a wooden table and chairs stood opposite and at the back of the room cups and plates were stacked on shelves. A large black pot, from which there came an enticing smell, hung over the fire. Jacob had no doubt that it contained food and he grew quite weak at the thought.

The woman told them to sit at the table. Then she placed bowls in front of them, filled with a thick brown liquid in which solid pieces were floating. The word 'stew' came into Jacob's mind. It was very hot with an earthy sort of taste and it satisfied their hunger much more effectively than the food they had been given in Locus. The woman herself did not eat, however. Instead she watched them intently.

When they had eaten, she took the pot off the fire and replaced it with another. This one she filled with water from the bucket Jacob had carried indoors. She covered the pot and brought out a large jug into which she placed a handful of dried leaves. When she was satisfied that the water in the pot was hot enough, she poured it over the leaves. Soon the smell of stew was replaced by a different, fresher fragrance.

'It's tea,' Aysha said.

The woman nodded. She poured the tea into cups and while they sipped it she told them that her name was Nemain and they introduced themselves in turn.

'What brings you here?' she asked.

'We're looking for the Palace of Remembrance,' Aysha told her. 'Do you know where we can find it?'

Nemain shook her head. 'I'm sorry, I can't help you,' she said. 'I never go far from the river.'

'But surely you would have heard of it if it was nearby?' Toby said.

The woman shrugged. 'I see no one and I hear nothing,' she told him, 'only the sound of the river.'

Jacob was not sure he believed her. Hadn't she mentioned something earlier about a man who came with the clothes? He would have liked to ask her a great many more questions but he was dreadfully tired from a day spent wandering in the wilderness with nothing to eat and it was all he could do to keep his eyes open.

Seeing how sleepy her guests were, Nemain went out of the house and returned a few minutes later with a huge bundle of dried grass which she threw on the floor in a corner of the room. 'You can sleep on this,' she told them. Then she bade them goodnight and disappeared into another room.

Jacob looked at the others. 'What do you think?' he asked.

'I don't know,' Aysha said. 'I don't think I trust her.'

'Neither do I,' Toby said. 'But right now I'm too tired to care.'

They lay down on the dried grass and were asleep almost as soon as they had closed their eyes. Much later, however, Jacob woke to find himself in total darkness, except for the light given off by the glowing embers of the fire. He had no idea where he was at first, but the feel of the dried grass brought it all back. He could hear the other two breathing and as his eyes adjusted to the darkness, he could make out their shapes lying on the floor beside him. He thought about the conversation they had had with Nemain and wished he had asked her more questions. Tomorrow he would try to talk to her properly, he decided. With this thought, he closed his eyes and went back to sleep.

The next time he woke it was morning. The front door stood open and daylight flooded the room. The fire was burning brightly again and Nemain was standing over it, cooking something in the big black pot. It didn't smell like stew this time. He sat up and stretched. Beside him, Toby and Aysha stirred.

'Good morning,' he said.

Nemain merely grunted.

Jacob tried again. 'Thank you for feeding us and for letting us stay the night,' he said.

Nemain nodded. 'Today you can gather firewood,' she told him.

She took out the bowls they had eaten from the previous night and filled them with a creamy brown substance which she spooned out of the pot. 'It's time for breakfast,' she announced.

This meal was completely different from the one they had eaten the night before. The creamy brown substance tasted sweet and its texture was grainy. No name for it came into Jacob's head and he wondered whether it was something unique to this place.

This time Nemain joined in the meal. She ate quickly and noisily. Food dribbled down the side of her mouth and she wiped it away with her sleeve. As soon as her bowl was empty, she stood up and looked at the others expectantly until they, too, had finished. 'Now you must help me gather firewood,' she told them.

She led them outside towards a wooded area not far from the house. The ground here was littered with dead branches and it was clear that collecting firewood would not be a difficult task. 'Make a pile here,' she told them. 'I'll come back to see how you're getting on. Now I must do some washing.'

'I feel as if I'm working for Berith again,' Toby observed as they set about picking up the fallen branches. But he meant it only as a joke. This was nothing like stone-picking. They were there of their own free will and they could have walked away at any point. Besides, it was a pleasant day and there was something very satisfying about building the pile of firewood.

They must have worked for at least an hour before Nemain returned to inspect the pile. Grudgingly, she agreed that it was large enough. Then she showed them where to put it and went back to her work.

There was already an enormous pile of wood behind the house and they stacked their bundles on top of this. 'She must have spent a long time gathering it,' Toby observed.

'Do you think anyone else helps her?' Aysha asked.

'I wondered about that,' Jacob replied. 'I got the impression when we first arrived that she sees someone from Locus regularly.'

'Then we'd better not stay here too long,' Toby pointed out.

'I'd just like to ask her a few more questions before we leave,' Jacob said. 'I think she knows more than she's telling us.'

When they had finished bringing the wood down to the house they went to find Nemain and discovered her kneeling beside the river, washing clothes. Those already washed were spread out on some nearby stones to dry but there was a huge pile still to wash. It was clear that they were not her clothes. There were far too many. What struck Jacob, as he looked at them, was the colours. There were blues and reds and greens, even purples; there was not a black dress among them. Nor was there a grey uniform, though he was sure Nemain had said something about the clothes coming from Locus. 'We've finished stacking the firewood,' Toby told her. 'We thought we might get on our way again.'

Nemain looked at him. She nodded her head wearily.

'You've got an awful lot of clothes to wash,' Aysha observed.

Nemain sighed. 'They never stop bringing them,' she said. 'And some of them are so difficult to get clean.'

Jacob was about to ask who never stopped bringing them when he suddenly paused. Surely he recognised the clothes that were soaking in the water? There was a pair of blue trousers and a dark green T-shirt, both of which seemed incredibly familiar. Beside them was a red sweater. All three had the same irregular brown markings on them. A feeling of intense anxiety began to overwhelm him as Nemain reached into the water, picked up the red sweater and held it up. 'Look at this,' she complained. 'How am I supposed to get the blood out of it?'

Her words seemed to hang in the silence. Slowly Jacob turned and looked at Aysha. She was staring at Nemain with an expression of complete horror on her face. 'It's the same with these,' Nemain continued, picking up the trousers. 'Look at the stains. They'll never come out.'

It was too much for Jacob to bear. He began backing

away, shaking his head. He had to get out of there. That was all he could think of as Nemain carried on holding up the clothes, apparently quite unaware of his reaction. 'What am I supposed to do with them?' she repeated. 'They're covered in blood.' Jacob could stand it no longer. He turned and ran as fast as he could. He could hear the others following close behind but he did not once look back.

14. THE VALLEY OF BONES

'We drank from that river,' Aysha said. They were the first words she had spoken for at least an hour. The three of them were sitting with their backs to a large rock. All around was flat, open country. They had covered a great deal of ground since that morning; the river and Nemain were far behind them now.

'We didn't know,' Jacob said.

Aysha made no reply.

'What do you think it meant?' Toby asked. Of the three, he was the least disturbed by what they had seen. Understandably, since his clothes had not been among those in the water.

Jacob shrugged. He had been asking himself the same question over and over again.

'Maybe we would have been better off if we'd stayed in Locus,' Jacob said bitterly.

'Don't say that,' Toby told him. He spoke gently but firmly.

'But what if we're making a terrible mistake?' Jacob went on. 'Because that's what I'm beginning to suspect. All this time I've been thinking that if I could just get my old life back everything would be wonderful but now it looks like my old life might have been worse than this one.'

Toby thought about this for a long time. Then he said, 'When you first suggested we leave Locus, I didn't really want to go.'

'You told us that,' Jacob said.

'Yes but I didn't tell you why,' Toby replied. 'Before you arrived in Locus I had this really strong memory, the most vivid one I've ever had.'

'What was it about?' Aysha asked.

'I was lying in a hospital bed,' Toby went on, 'and I was watching a moth flying round and round a light. The moth kept bashing against the light bulb and I thought, why doesn't it stop? But it didn't. And at the same time there was this pain inside me. It went on and on, like the moth, and I knew that wasn't going to stop either.' As he spoke, his eyes were full of the memory of that pain.

Jacob looked at him in bewilderment. 'So why do you want your old life back?' he asked.

'Because I want to know who I really am,' Toby said. 'I want the truth, even if it's nothing but suffering. You two made me want that. And I'm not letting you give up now.'

Aysha got up and went over to him. She put her arms around him and hugged him. 'Thank you, Toby,' she said.

They sat in silence for a long time after that, lost in their own thoughts. Despite what Toby had said, the sight of Nemain holding up the bloodstained clothing still filled Jacob's mind. He thought about the fact that he had worn those clothes and not even recognised the stains for what they were and he wondered what other dreadful secrets lay waiting to be discovered.

Suddenly he felt Aysha grip his arm. 'We're being watched,' she hissed. 'Don't do anything in a hurry. Just turn your head very slowly to the left.'

Jacob did as she told him and the reason for her whispered command was immediately clear. Some distance away a group of savage-looking dogs were staring in their direction.

'Do you see them?' Aysha whispered.

'Yes,' Jacob and Toby said together.

'What are we going to do?'

'Get up very slowly and start walking away,' Jacob suggested.

The other two nodded.

'I'm going to count to three and then we'll all get up together,' Jacob went on. 'One, two, three.'

The three of them stood up. Instantly the dogs began racing in their direction. 'Run!' Jacob shouted.

They ran as hard and as fast as they could but within no time the dogs were almost at their heels. 'Split up!' Jacob shouted and the three of them began running in different directions. The dogs didn't hesitate. They split up, too.

Jacob knew that he had to find somewhere to hide and he had to do so very quickly. He could not keep running for very much longer. Every breath was painful but he forced himself onwards. The dog should have leapt on him by now but it seemed content to remain just behind him, snapping at his ankles every now and again but not sinking its teeth into his flesh. Then he realised what it was doing. It was waiting for him to collapse. It was just running along comfortably in his wake, letting him exhaust himself, allowing him to do the work. Then, once he had stumbled and fallen to the ground, all it would need to do would be to tear open his throat. He could turn and face it, of course, but he knew what the result of that confrontation would be. He was weak already from lack of food and water. The dog, on the other hand, looked very familiar with this sort of territory. It was very big, with cruel eyes and a mouth full of yellow teeth. He would be no match for an animal like that. His only chance was to get away from it, to lose it somehow.

He needed to find a tree or even a patch of high ground which the dog wouldn't be able to climb, but he was running in the wrong direction. They had left the hilly, wooded area near the river far behind them. Up ahead the land was flat and featureless. As he ran, he desperately scanned the horizon for something that would help him. To his left, there was a line of bushes. It wasn't very promising but perhaps it would lead to more vegetation or there might be something there that he could use as a weapon. He changed his course, heading towards it, all the time wondering how much longer he could keep this up.

There was a sharp pain in his side and he could hear himself gasping for breath as he ran and he knew that he sounded like a creature reaching the end of its strength. Undoubtedly that was what the dog heard, too.

The line of shrubs was very close now and he saw, to his dismay, that there was nothing here that could help him: no trees, no rocks to climb, nothing but thorny branches to tear at his skin as he plunged through their midst and tough trailing creepers that extended rope-like tentacles and threatened to trip him up. There were tears pouring down his face because he knew that he would have to stop at any moment now. His body was failing him even though his will still burnt as strongly as ever.

Then suddenly the ground seemed to disappear beneath him. His arms and legs flailed about desperately as he tried to keep running but he was falling. There was a second or two when he realised that he had run off the end of a cliff. Then he hit the ground.

He was not dead. That was the first thing he realised when he opened his eyes. The fall had not killed him. He had landed on soft, sandy earth and perhaps that was why he was still in one piece. But his whole body ached, especially his head. He sat up gingerly and looked back at the cliff down which he had fallen. Actually, to call it a cliff was to exaggerate. It was more like a shelf of rock.

He tried to get up and felt a stab of pain in his ankle. He wondered if it was broken and tried flexing it. He could move it back and forth so he suspected that it was still intact. He began gently massaging it and after a while the pain subsided a little. He tried getting to his feet again and found that this was possible, though still painful.

There was no sign of the dog. That was one thing to be grateful for, at least. However, there was also no sign of Toby or Aysha. This thought filled him with a sense of panic. He called out their names at the top of his voice but no reply was forthcoming. He tried again and again but there was only silence in return. Dismayed, he began to limp along the base of the rocky shelf, looking to see whether there was a way he could climb back up, since Toby and Aysha must be somewhere in that direction. But it seemed to be just as steep all the way along its length. In fact, the further he went, the more like a real cliff it became until the prospect of climbing began to seem quite impossible.

His ankle was hurting dreadfully. He sat down on the ground and tried to decide what he should do next. But the more he considered his position, the worse it seemed. He was utterly exhausted, he had no idea where he was, no food and nothing to drink and he had lost his companions. He did not even know which way he ought to be facing to continue his journey. However, this was the least of his worries since the whole idea of the Palace of Remembrance now seemed like a cruel joke. He would have wept but he lacked the energy. Instead he sat, with his knees drawn up and his head in his hands, telling himself that he might as well die here as anywhere.

His thoughts were interrupted by a cough. He looked up and saw, to his surprise, the most peculiar figure standing just out of reach, looking at him with frank curiosity. It was a skinny, half-naked old man. He had long, matted white hair and a scraggy beard, and his only clothing was a collection of necklaces and what looked like an animal skin tied around his waist. He seemed wizened by age, as if weather and time had long ago dried him up completely. But there was an intensity about his gaze that was almost animal-like. He coughed again, and spat on the ground.

'Who are you?' Jacob asked.

The old man looked startled. He had clearly not expected Jacob to speak. Now he frowned, as if he was not sure how to reply. Then, speaking in a surprisingly strong voice, he said, 'Moloch.'

'Moloch,' Jacob repeated. 'That's your name, is it?'

The old man pointed to himself. 'Moloch,' he said again.

'I'm Jacob.'

'Ja-cob,' Moloch said, pronouncing the name as if it were two words.

'I need food and water,' Jacob told him. 'Can you help me?'

Moloch nodded. 'Maybe,' he said.

'And I need to find my friends,' Jacob went on. 'I came here with two other people, a boy and a girl. Have you seen them?'

Moloch shook his head. 'Moloch sees no one else,' he said, 'only Ja-cob.'

'We were chased by wild dogs,' Jacob went on, 'and we got split up.'

'Dogs very dangerous,' Moloch agreed. He drew his finger across his throat. 'Kill you easily.'

Jacob had no difficulty believing this. He wondered anxiously about Aysha and Toby. Would they have managed to get away from the dogs?

'I need to look for my friends,' he said. 'Will you help me?'

Moloch looked doubtful. 'First eat,' he said, 'then look.'

It was very hard to simply abandon the search for his friends but Jacob knew it made sense. If he kept wandering about in the wilderness without food, he would just collapse from hunger and that would be no help to anyone.

'OK,' he agreed. 'Will you show me where I can get some food?'

Moloch seemed to think about this. Then he said, 'You give me something first.'

Jacob was dismayed by this answer. What could he possibly trade with this strange old man? 'I'm sorry but I haven't got anything to give you,' he said.

Moloch pointed to Jacob's shoes.

'You want my shoes?' Jacob asked in disbelief.

Moloch nodded eagerly.

Jacob was not at all happy about the idea of parting with his shoes but he was in no position to argue. Reluctantly he took them off and handed them over.

Moloch accepted the shoes but then pointed to Jacob's socks.

'You want my socks as well?'

Moloch nodded again.

Jacob sighed. He peeled off his socks. Moloch took them, then sat on the ground. Slowly and clumsily he put on the socks, followed by the shoes. When he had completed this operation, he seemed enormously pleased with himself.

'You have to tie the laces,' Jacob told him.

Moloch looked baffled.

Jacob bent down and tied the laces for him. This seemed to please Moloch even more. He stood up and capered about, laughing to himself, like a little child. Then, seemingly satisfied, he nodded to Jacob. 'Come,' he said.

He began to walk away from the cliff, setting off across the sandy plain that stretched like a bowl between the shelf of rock down which Jacob had fallen earlier and another line of cliffs in the distance.

Jacob followed, wincing every time his feet came into contact with sharp stones. 'Is that where you live?' he asked, pointing towards the cliffs that faced them.

'Yes,' Moloch told him. 'Not far. You see.'

It looked a very long way to Jacob but he had no choice but to limp along after Moloch. After a while he asked, 'Have you heard of the Palace of Remembrance?'

Moloch nodded. 'Yes,' he said.

Jacob's first reaction was surprise. He had almost ceased to believe in the palace himself. He studied the old man carefully, trying to judge whether or not he was telling the truth. It was hard to tell but he seemed sincere enough. Perhaps this whole journey had not been a waste of time after all. 'Can you show me the way there?' Jacob asked.

'Maybe,' Moloch agreed. 'First you eat.'

'Thank you,' Jacob said.

As they continued across the plain, Jacob noticed a peculiar phenomenon. The ground ahead of them seemed to be littered with white stones that gleamed dully in the afternoon sun, causing the whole plain to shimmer. He thought of asking Moloch about this but judged it wiser to save his energy for the journey. Instead he focused on putting one foot in front of the other and keeping up with Moloch.

Even so, their progress was slow because, despite his determination, Jacob had to keep pausing to rest. On one occasion, while he was sitting on the ground trying to summon up enough strength to continue, Moloch, who was crouching nearby, suddenly shot out a hand and seized something. Looking very pleased with himself he held it out towards Jacob. It was an insect, long and black, its legs waving frantically between Moloch's finger and thumb. Jacob was unsure how he was supposed to react. Was he expected to congratulate Moloch for being so clever in catching it? Moloch waited for a moment, then he shrugged, put the insect in his mouth, chewed briefly, and swallowed it.

So that was it. Moloch had been offering him something to eat. Well, it was not Jacob's idea of food: even less appetising than the spongy white food they were served each day in Locus. He shuddered, hoping that whatever else there might be to eat when they reached Moloch's house would be more attractive than this.

'Come,' Moloch said, when he had finished his morsel. He was impatient to be moving, shifting from foot to foot whenever he had to wait, often looking over his shoulder, as if he feared anyone discovering him there. Jacob would have liked to remain where he was for a great deal longer but he got up reluctantly and followed.

A little while later, they began to reach the area that had seemed to Jacob to be littered with white stones. Now he realised that what he had taken for stones were actually bones. Hundreds and hundreds of them, scattered across the plain, like leaves torn from a tree in autumn. And as he looked more closely he saw, to his horror, that here and there human skulls nestled amongst them.

'How did all these bones get here?' he asked.

'Many people killed here. Long, long ago,' Moloch told him.

'Who were they?' Jacob asked.

Moloch seemed to think about this for a long time. Finally he said, 'Wandering people. Dedanim.'

Jacob struggled to understand what he had just heard. These were the people whom he had ridden alongside, the men and women with whom he had eaten and from whom he had escaped, the inhabitants of his dream. Yet they had died so long ago that even Moloch could scarcely remember them.

'Who killed them?' he asked, after a while.

Moloch spread his hands in a gesture of uncertainty. 'Enemies,' he said. 'Or maybe they fight themselves. Who knows? Afterwards, everyone dead. Only bones left.' As he said this he suddenly grinned, bent forwards and picked something up from the ground. Looking immensely pleased with himself, he held it up. Jacob expected to see another insect struggling between his fingers, but he now saw that what Moloch held was a tooth. At the same time he noticed that what he had taken for beads on the necklaces that adorned Moloch's throat were in fact human teeth, four or five separate strings of them. Presumably they had all been picked up from this dusty plain in the same way. At least Jacob hoped this was the case, although he didn't feel entirely confident. Moloch was probably not to be trusted, he decided.

It was getting towards evening when they finally reached the cliffs on the other side of the plain. Moloch led the way to a door set in the base of the cliff. It was made out of a number of small tree trunks lashed together vertically and the whole thing was fixed by what looked like leather hinges to another, larger tree trunk hammered into the ground. A big rock in front of the door kept it in position. With a grunt, Moloch pushed this aside and the door swung open, revealing the entrance to a cave.

'In,' Moloch said, gesturing with his hand for Jacob to step into the cave.

Jacob peered uncertainly inside. The interior of the cave was in darkness and it was hard to make out anything at all. Perhaps it would be wiser to let Moloch go in first, he decided. Suddenly he felt something hit him very hard in the back. He cried out and stumbled forward into the darkness, tripping and landing on his hands and knees on the floor. He scarcely had time to realise what was happening when the door shut and he was in pitch darkness.

'No!' he shouted, scrambling to his feet and running towards the cracks of light that showed around the door. But he was too late. Moloch had already managed to replace the rock which held it in place.

'Open this door!' Jacob shouted, pushing as hard as he could. But he was exhausted and weak from hunger and his efforts made no difference. He paused to collect his strength, then set his shoulder against the door, dug his heels into the ground and shoved with all his might. At first it seemed as if he had a chance. The crack of light beside the door began to widen very slightly. Then suddenly something hit the other side of the door heavily, causing the whole thing to shudder, and he realised that somehow or other Moloch had managed to move a much larger boulder into place against the door.

'Let me out of here!' he shouted, hammering with his fists on the door, but he knew it was no good. Moloch was probably already out of hearing. Exhausted, he slumped to the floor and accepted defeat.

15. IN THE HEART OF THE HILL

He had no idea how much time had passed while he had been asleep. It could have been minutes, it could have been hours. His first thought was how hungry he was. His stomach felt as if something was gnawing at it from the inside. But he knew there was no point in dwelling on that. He had to get out of here while he still had some strength left and that meant thinking clearly. First of all he needed to understand exactly what had happened to him.

Why had Moloch locked him in the cave? What was the point? What else did he want from Jacob, apart from his shoes? He remembered the way the old man's hand had suddenly snaked out and seized the beetle. He had popped the creature into his mouth without the slightest qualm, as if he ate insects every day. Perhaps he did. In which case eating Jacob would probably make a very pleasant change. For that was certainly his intention. Jacob had no doubt about it now. He had been pushed into the cave to die of hunger and thirst and when he was dead, Moloch would make a meal of him. That was the plan. It wasn't terribly sophisticated but then neither was Moloch. He was vicious, malevolent and crafty, certainly, but he was not sophisticated. Jacob felt certain that he was cleverer than Moloch. And that thought gave him hope. He wasn't beaten yet. There might be a way of getting out of this.

Then he remembered that the tree trunks that made up the door were held together by some kind of rope. Maybe he could find something that would cut through it. A sharp stone might do. It would take a very long time because the rope was very thick but it might work. The trouble was it was so difficult to see anything in here. He felt around on the floor and his hands encountered a hard object. He picked it up. It felt like a long, smooth stick. He held it as close to his eyes as possible. Then, with horror, he realised what it was: a bone. He threw it away in disgust. For all he knew it might have been the remains of the last person whom Moloch had trapped.

He continued to search the floor of the cave, moving about on all fours. But nothing suitable came to hand, only more bones. To his surprise it seemed to be a little lighter at the back of the cave and it was not long before he discovered the reason. There was a small opening in the rear wall at about chest height. Some sort of tunnel seemed to lead diagonally upwards into the hill. Jacob craned his neck to look up it and there, at the very end, he could see a little square of light.

Immediately, a surge of hope filled him. The light could only be coming from the outside world. If he could climb along the tunnel, he might be able to get out. But it wouldn't be easy. The tunnel was very long and looked barely wide enough for Jacob to force his body into it. He would be like a worm, burrowing its way through the earth. More worrying than this was another thought which nagged away at him as he considered his plan. What if the tunnel got narrower? What if he found himself stuck halfway? Would he finish his days entombed in the heart of the hill?

For a long time he waited, balancing one fear against another, but at last he made up his mind to try. What else could he do? The alternative was to sit on the floor of the cave and starve. He counted to three, just to help himself build up the necessary courage. Then he put his arms out in front of him, like a diver, and wriggled his way into the tunnel.

It was not easy to make progress. He had to shuffle along, using his elbows against the sides to lever his body forward. This soon proved exhausting and he paused to rest. He was dreadfully uncomfortable and he cursed Moloch. He told himself that he should never have trusted him, that he had known from the moment he saw the old man there was something unpleasant about him, the way his eyes had seemed so much more alive than the rest of him, but not like human eyes, more like the eyes of some animal.

For some reason this made him think of the dream he had had in the dormitory and then, later, when they had first set out on their search for the Palace of Remembrance. Afterwards, on each occasion, he had scarcely been able to remember anything about the events he had witnessed; but now he clearly recalled the bird that had sat on the wire fence, its bright eyes peering in his direction. It had opened its mouth and released a stream of liquid notes. He could almost hear that song again and the thought of it cheered him, even here lying with his face pressed against the cold rock and the roof of the tunnel oppressively close to his head. Taking courage from this memory, he forced himself onwards again.

But it was very slow progress and his elbows began to hurt where the skin was rubbed raw by the sides of the tunnel. Meanwhile the little window of light in the distance seemed to get no closer. He continued to shuffle upwards, trying to keep his mind off the growing sense of claustrophobia by thinking about his dream and wondering what it meant. He was convinced it had something to do with his life before Locus and that it was a significant moment in that life. If only he could remember what came after it. But as he was wondering about this he became aware that something had changed. There seemed to be a little more light in the tunnel, somehow. A moment later fear gripped him so tightly that he could not move, as he became aware that someone was shouting at the base of the tunnel. He could not make out the words. Nor was there room for him to turn his head and look behind him, but it didn't matter. He had no difficulty recognising the voice. It was Moloch. He had come back, either to see whether Jacob was still alive, or simply to gloat. In either case he had been sorely disappointed. That much was obvious from the tone of his voice. He continued shouting up the tunnel and now Jacob could make out the words, 'Come back!' He continued wriggling along the tunnel as rapidly as he could.

After the initial outburst there was silence but Jacob did not allow himself to relax. For all he knew, Moloch had entered the tunnel and was even now scrambling towards him. Frantically he worked his way forward, ignoring the pain in his elbows and knees. But now another problem presented itself. The tunnel was getting narrower. He had suspected this for some time but had not even dared to think about it. Now he could ignore it no longer. The roof was definitely sloping downwards. If this continued he would find himself stuck, just as he had feared. He stopped, torn between two equal terrors.

As he hesitated, he began to notice an odd smell, but one that was definitely familiar. He sniffed, trying to decide what it was. The smell was getting stronger by the second. At the same time, he realised that the tunnel was getting darker. Had Moloch closed the door to the cave again, he wondered? Suddenly he realised what was causing both the smell and the growing darkness. Smoke. The tunnel behind him had been gradually filling up with smoke and now it was beginning to reach him. Wisps of it drifted past.

Frantically, Jacob squirmed forward. The roof of the tunnel was only inches above his head now but he had no choice — he had to drive himself onwards. However, he found, to his relief, that the tunnel did not become completely impassable. In fact it soon began widening again. That was some comfort, at least; but the smoke was getting worse. He coughed repeatedly and his eyes watered so much that he had to keep them shut. He could taste the smoke in his mouth, feel it wrapping itself around his body, but still he kept going.

He no longer thought about anything at all. His mind had become nothing but a focused point of willpower, driving him onwards like some blind creature that spends its life beneath the earth. He tried to take shallow breaths to prevent himself coughing and he kept his eyes firmly closed. When, after a long time he opened them, he was surprised to find that the window of light had grown perceptibly larger. It also seemed as if the air was less tainted with smoke. He must be a great deal nearer the outside world. Heartened, he continued to crawl forward. The old man's plan was not working. Moloch must have hoped that Jacob would give up and slide back down into his clutches. Well Jacob was stronger than that. Even though his body had scarcely any strength left in it, his will had not surrendered. He had refused to be a victim. He would carry on going his own way whatever obstacles he met.

These thoughts caused a feeling of exhilaration to bubble up in him and he found himself laughing out loud at his victory over Moloch, laughter that soon turned into a desperate coughing fit, leaving him too weak to move for a few minutes. But then he was off again, worming his way towards what was obviously the end of the tunnel.

In a few moments he would be outside, he told himself, standing on the bare hillside, breathing fresh air. He would have to be careful, of course. Moloch might well know where the tunnel came out. He might even be waiting by the exit. Jacob would have to proceed with extreme caution. All the same, the thought that his terrible ordeal was coming to an end made him feel quite light-headed.

Now, at last, he had reached the exit to the tunnel. It still seemed quite dark and gloomy outside. Could it be night-time? He had no idea how long he had been asleep in the cave. He pushed his head out of the tunnel and looked around. At first he could not understand where he was. Then gradually the truth dawned and a crushing feeling of disappointment descended upon him. The tunnel had not come out on the hillside at all. Instead it had ended in a much larger chamber inside the hill. He had struggled all this way from one cave into another.

He crawled out and lay on the ground, too weary to move another inch. The exultation he had felt about defeating Moloch drained away. He felt utterly empty, as if his body was no more than a husk and the real Jacob had gone far away.

And yet after he had lain like that for a long time, some force inside his brain began dragging him back to the here and now. A thought was forming in the back of his mind, a thought that demanded his attention. What was it, he wondered irritably? Why did he have to keep going on like this? Why could he not just give up, close his eyes and die? But his will to live was still too strong. And that will was demanding that he concentrate now, that he focus his mind. Upon what, he asked himself wearily? The answer came back immediately: upon the fact that this chamber had been the source of the light he had glimpsed when he first looked along the tunnel; upon the fact that, although it was gloomy in here, it was still bright enough to see. Which could only mean one thing. Somehow or other this cave must be connected to the outside world. With a groan he realised that his struggle was not over yet. There was still the chance of a way out and he must find it.

Slowly he got up off the ground and looked about him. The light was coming from one side of the chamber, and he went over to investigate more closely. Looking upwards, he could see a square of daylight far above him. And by its light he could make out a series of metal staples that had been driven into the wall to make a primitive ladder. It was clear that this was the way he must go. But it was so high.

The sight made him feel almost physically sick. He pictured himself climbing up the side of the cavern and found himself remembering Stefan's story about an insect trying to climb up the wall of the dormitory. It had got so far and then fallen off but had immediately begun again. This process had been repeated over and over again until the struggle had been ended by someone who had come through the doorway and stepped on the creature as it lay on the ground, struggling to right itself. That was what happened to those who struggled against the odds. Someone put them out of their misery by treading on them.

There was no point in thoughts like this. He knew that. However much the prospect frightened him, he would have to climb the ladder. The longer he spent thinking about it, the harder it would get. He took a deep breath, then gripping a rung with both hands, he placed his foot on the first step of the ladder and began the long climb towards daylight.

From the very start he realised that he should not look down. It was an instinctive knowledge. He couldn't remember climbing to any great height before, but perhaps he had done so in his previous life. Whatever the case, he knew that he must not peer back over his shoulder. The only way was to keep putting his hand up to seize the staple above, then stepping onto the next rung of the ladder. It was best not to think about what he was doing at all. Of course he had to be careful, to make sure his grip was firm and his foothold secure, but apart from that it was important to just proceed mechanically. Because if he began to think about what was involved, his whole body would start to shake, he would lose his fragile grip on the ladder and go tumbling down through the gloom onto the cold stone below.

At first he tried counting the rungs as a way of keeping calm but after he had reached two hundred, even this began to make him anxious. Instead he tried to focus on all the good things that had happened to him since waking up in the field beside the river. He remembered how he had stood in the dormitory for the first time looking round at a room full of strangers, feeling completely intimidated, until Toby had taken him under his wing. He remembered, too, how he and Aysha had found comfort against the fierce cold of the night by lying with their arms around each other. Where were Toby and Aysha now, he wondered? He desperately hoped they were still alive, that they hadn't been torn to pieces by the wild dogs.

Although he had stopped consciously counting the rungs, some part of his mind must have continued to do so automatically, because he was aware that he had passed six hundred by now and still the window of light seemed a long way away. His ankle was hurting him desperately and he wondered whether he had managed to get halfway. Despite the warning voices telling him that it was a mistake, Jacob could not resist the temptation to look over his shoulder and see how far he had come.

He could not see the bottom of the cavern at all. Instead, he seemed to be suspended in an endless, gloomy vault. A sickening dizziness took hold of him and he felt an unreasoning urge to let go of the ladder and fall into the darkness. He broke into a cold sweat and his legs trembled so that he felt certain they would give way under him. A voice seemed to be whispering in his mind that the easiest thing to do was to give up, that it was just a matter of straightening out his fingers, of letting his body relax. It would be like going to sleep, the whisper assured him. There would be no pain, just a sense of speed, then an instantaneous forgetting.

It was time to decide, he told himself. He could not just stay here halfway between the darkness and the light. He needed to go one way or the other and he was not sure he could face the rest of the climb. His body was so weary and the thought of letting go was comforting. Yes, that was what he needed to do. That would be for the best. He was just about to release his hold when it occurred to him that he had heard this phrase before. Where, he wondered? Then into his mind came the vision of his mother and his father quarrelling. He remembered his mother saying, 'I think we should spend some time apart.' His father had looked at her for a long time. Then he had sighed. 'Is that what you really want?' he had asked. 'I think it might be for the best,' she had replied. But she had been wrong. He had been certain of that then. He was equally certain of it now. And with that certainty came the memory of why he was doing all this, of what it was that had made him set out on his search for the Palace of Remembrance in the first place. He had wanted to get back to the land of the living so that he could do something to help his parents, so that they could see that splitting up was not for the best, that it was a terrible mistake, like dropping off a ladder onto a cold stone floor when you could be climbing upwards towards the light. He turned back to the wall, took hold of the next rung and resumed his climb.

Step by step, rung by rung, he moved upwards until he could feel a breeze upon his face and smell the outside world. Now there was no longer any need for him to drive himself onwards, the scent of freedom was enough. His body seemed to have acquired a new strength at the prospect of once again standing beneath the sky and breathing fresh air. At last there were only a few rungs left. He hesitated for a moment. Would Moloch be waiting for him?

Bracing himself for some sort of attack, he very cautiously pushed his head out of the entrance. He had emerged on the other side of the hill, as he had expected. To his relief he saw that there was no sign of Moloch. All around him there was green grass, the smell of which was like some wonderful, exotic perfume. And further down the slope he could see an enormous building.

His heart leapt at the sight. It had to be the Palace of Remembrance.

16. THE PALACE OF REMEMBRANCE

The grey stone building rose into the sky like some natural phenomenon, as if it had not been built but had rather grown out of the hillside. At its centre was a great tower that ended in a windowless dome. Two great wings of the building projected on each side and a path led between them to the front entrance. Timidly, Jacob made his way along this path.

A great iron knocker hung on the front door. He picked it up and let it fall heavily, its crash disturbing the silence that hung over the whole place. He waited for a long time after the echoes had died away but there was no response. Just as he was on the point of picking up the knocker again, the door swung open and he gazed on a familiar face.

'It seems you have found me at last,' Virgil said.

Jacob was too surprised to do any more than nod.

'You'd better come in,' Virgil continued. 'No sense in hanging around on the threshold.'

He led the way along a gloomy passage. Burning torches had been placed at intervals and by their light Jacob could see that the walls were covered with paintings in which long processions of people, some wearing crowns and jewels, others dressed shabbily, were being led by strange creatures, half-human, half-animal. One had the head of a dog, another the body of a serpent. A skeleton banging a drum danced in front of them.

'Come along,' Virgil said impatiently, as Jacob stopped to stare. 'Their majesties are waiting for you. It would not be wise to keep them waiting.'

A moment later they stopped in front of a door. 'Wait in here with the others,' he said. He opened the door and Jacob stepped inside. He briefly took in the fact that the room was richly decorated with more complicated pictures on the walls, before he realised that sitting on chairs at a table in the middle of the room were Toby and Aysha. They broke into smiles when they saw him. Aysha sprang to her feet and threw her arms around him. 'Jacob!' she said. 'We thought something terrible must have happened to you.'

'Something terrible did happen to me,' he replied, 'in fact a lot of terrible things happened to me. But I survived.'

'Sit down and tell us all about it,' Aysha suggested.

Jacob sat down and told them about his fall and about meeting Moloch. He described the ordeal that had followed, including his journey through the tunnel and up the ladder.

'Our story is nothing like as bad as that,' Toby told him. 'We found a tree. It must have been the only tree for miles around but there it was. We just climbed up into it. I don't know how we did it. I've certainly never done anything so fast before. Anyway once we were up there we just waited for the dogs to get bored, which took hours. But in the end they got up and wandered off. Then we looked for you but we couldn't find you. We didn't know what to do. We

159

thought you must have been killed. Then we saw Virgil coming towards us.'

'You met him out there, in the wilderness?' Jacob asked, in surprise.

'Yes.'

'Our first instinct was to turn and run,' Aysha added, 'but, to tell you the truth, we were just too exhausted. We'd made up our minds that he could take us back to Locus if he wanted to. We'd had enough. So we just stood there waiting for him. But when he arrived all he said was, "Where's Jacob?" We said we didn't know and he said you always were a difficult boy. Then he brought us here.' She paused. Then she added, 'I'm glad you made it.'

'I nearly didn't,' Jacob replied.

As he said this the door opened and Virgil stepped into the room. 'Their majesties will see you one at a time,' he announced. 'They will begin with you,' he added, pointing to Aysha. She got up, gave the other two a little nervous wave and followed Virgil back into the corridor.

'What do you think they'll say to us?' Toby asked.

Jacob shrugged.

'I mean, do you think they'll let us go back to the land of the living?' Toby went on.

'I don't know. Maybe they don't have the power. Maybe they'll just send us back to Locus.'

'If they do, I'm not going,' Toby said, fiercely.

Jacob smiled, remembering the boy who had confessed that he lacked the courage to carry on without the support of his friends. 'At least it won't be long before we find out one way or the other,' he said.

After that neither of them said much more until Virgil put his head around the door again. This time he beckoned Toby and Jacob was left by himself. Now that he was alone, he realised that he ought to think about what he was going to say to the king and queen. He needed to put his case carefully, he decided. He would say it was unfair that he should have been robbed of his memory, taken from his friends, made to work picking up stones, given food that nourished but brought no pleasure, and finally forced to endure a journey through the wilderness to find someone to whom he could make his complaint. He would also explain that he needed to return to the world of the living, not just for his own sake but for his parents' sake as well.

When he was satisfied with his speech, he got up and studied the pictures on the walls. They showed more of the strange processions of people of all sorts. One wall in particular caught his attention. It showed an apparently endless line of children following a skeleton. 'That's us,' Jacob thought to himself, 'that's all the children of Locus.'

Just then he was disturbed by the sound of the door being opened again. 'Their majesties will see you now,' Virgil said.

Jacob followed him out of the room. There were a lot of questions he would have liked to ask Virgil but he felt sure that he was no more likely to get answers this time than on the first occasion they had met. Virgil led him down a carpeted corridor and stopped before a door on which the familiar two-faced symbol had been painted in gold. 'Here we are,' he said. He opened the door and motioned Jacob inside.

They were in an enormous room which seemed almost entirely empty, except for a long, thin black carpet leading from the doorway to a raised platform on which an old white-haired man was standing. He was dressed in black robes and wore a silver crown on his head.

'You may approach,' Virgil whispered to Jacob. Then he backed out of the door and disappeared.

Now that he had finally reached the person he had travelled all this way to meet, Jacob was reluctant to go forward and speak. What if he messed everything up at this final stage? But he could not stand by the door any longer. So, shaking, he walked slowly forward while the old man considered him severely out of watery grey eyes. 'Well then,' he said when Jacob had reached the dais, 'what is it that you want from me?' He spoke in a voice that sounded as ancient and as weary as time itself.

'Please, your majesty,' Jacob began, 'I want my life back.' He was aware, as he spoke, that he sounded more like a whining child than an elegant speech-maker but he could not help himself. His carefully thought-out words had vanished from his head. All he was left with was his raw desire to return to the world of the living.

The old man nodded his head but his grim expression did not change. 'Always the same,' he said. 'Always this yearning for what has been left behind. Sometimes it is better not to look backwards. Did that never occur to you?'

Jacob was uncertain how to reply. 'It isn't fair to keep me here,' he pointed out.

The old man raised one eyebrow. 'Not fair?' he said. 'Not fair!' He spoke as if the very idea filled him with indignation. 'Nothing is fair, Jacob. Do you not realise that? When you dwelt in the land of the living there were millions of children dying every day from disease, starvation and neglect. Was that fair?'

Jacob shook his head.

'Of course not,' the old man continued. 'It was simply an accident of birth, that is all. Who took any notice of them when they raised their hands and complained that life was not fair? No one. Least of all you.'

Jacob could think of nothing to say in reply. The king's accusation was no doubt true but how could he answer it when he could remember nothing about his earlier life.

The old man was silent for a long time, as if lost in thought. Finally he seemed to rouse himself. 'Well, you are here,' he said. 'You have reached my palace despite everything and I am obliged to consider what you have to say. But let us suppose for a moment that it is possible to turn back time. Let us suppose that I do have the power to send you back to the land of the living. Indeed, let us imagine that everything that has been lost could be reclaimed. Do you think the world would be a better place for that?' He fixed Jacob with a steely glare.

Jacob was not entirely certain what the question really meant but he nodded his head all the same. 'I think it could be,' he replied.

The old man sighed. 'Do you know what the most ridiculous thing about humanity is?' he demanded. But before Jacob could answer the king continued. 'Hope,' he declared. 'And it is the one thing that will not die. Let me explain something to you. People arrive in my kingdom for all sorts of reasons but in this case the decision to come here was yours alone.'

Jacob stared back at him in astonishment. What the king had said made no sense at all. 'Are you saying that I chose to come here?' he asked.

'Not exactly,' the king replied. 'But it was your decision that brought you here. And a very foolish decision it was, too. Yet if I were to return you to the land of the living, who is to say that you would not make exactly the same decision again?'

'I won't, I promise,' Jacob told him.

The old man gave a short, mirthless laugh. 'Many others have stood where you stand now and made that promise,' he declared. 'Very few have kept it. However, the matter is out of my hands now.'

Moving suddenly and swiftly, he turned around but, instead of the back of an old man, Jacob now confronted the face and body of a young woman. It was as if the two beings inhabited one body. She smiled at him. 'Do not be alarmed Jacob,' she told him. 'We each face opposite ways. He faces towards death and I face towards life. It is me you have been searching for all this time. Now listen to what I have to say. At the other end of this room is a door. In a moment you must open it and step through. Once you do so, you will have left this world entirely behind. You will be back in the land of the living. But wait,' she continued, when she saw the smile of joy that had begun to spread across Jacob's face. 'There is something you must understand. Once you have left my kingdom behind, whatever has happened to you in the land of the dead will be forgotten.'

'Does that mean I won't remember Aysha and Toby?' Jacob asked, in alarm.

The queen nodded her head. 'Should you meet them again, they will be strangers to you.'

Jacob was dismayed. He had not expected this. 'I will meet them again, won't I?' he demanded. 'You have sent them back to the land of the living, haven't you?'

The queen nodded gravely. 'Yes, I have sent them back to the land of the living,' she told him, 'but whether or not you will meet them again does not depend on me.'

'But don't you know what's going to happen to us?' Jacob demanded.

The queen shook her head. 'Though I can look past the borders of my kingdom, I cannot see very far. However, I will tell you this much: I believe it is likely your lives will be drawn together again but before that can happen you, Jacob, must earn the right to remain in the land of the living.'

Jacob looked at her in disbelief. 'What else do I have to do?' he asked. Surely his journey here earned him that right already?

'Listen carefully,' the queen continued. 'When you walk through that doorway, you will face the very same decision that brought you here in the first place and there is no guarantee that you will not make that same mistake again because the knowledge you have gained in death will be lost to you.'

Jacob struggled to understand what she was telling him. 'Does that mean I could end up back here again?' he asked. The idea was almost more horrible than anything that had happened so far.

The queen shook her head. 'No one passes through my kingdom more than once,' she told him.

'So what happens if I make the wrong decision?'

'There are many other kingdoms between life and death and each one is different. Are you still sure you wish to take your chance?'

The thought of all those other worlds was a daunting one but Jacob was not going to be discouraged. He had come too far. 'Yes,' he said. 'I'm quite sure.'

'Then I wish you good fortune. Perhaps what you have learned will stay with you in some way. Who can say?'

Jacob hesitated. There was still one question he needed to have answered. 'What about all the others?' he asked. 'The ones I left behind in Locus? Will they ever get out of here?'

'When they want to badly enough,' the queen replied. 'Not everyone goes back to the land of the living, Jacob, but nobody stays here for ever.'

'Even Stefan?'

'Stefan is at this moment thinking of leaving and he has you to thank for that.'

'Me?' Jacob began. 'But how . . .'

'Enough questions!' the queen told him. 'Leave this very instant or I shall change my mind.'

Jacob needed no further telling. He crossed the room, seized the handle of the door and opened it. A blinding light came from the other side and, shielding his eyes, he stepped forward to meet it.

17. BIRDSONG

As the 11.30 from Southampton to London raced along the line, a girl sat towards the rear of the train, drinking a carton of orange juice. She could have been anywhere between fourteen and sixteen. In her bright red sweater she stood out like a beacon among the other passengers. Her father sat beside her reading a newspaper he had found on the seat. He read slowly, mouthing the words to himself, since English was not his first language. The newspaper was a week old but he did not mind. He was engrossed in an article about a boy called Toby, the same age as his own daughter, who was undergoing revolutionary new surgery. Doctors estimated the boy's chances of survival at just fifty per cent. 'A lot depends on his own will to live,' the surgeon in charge of the operation was quoted as saying.

The man put down his newspaper and gazed fondly at his daughter. He was grateful that she was fit and healthy. The idea of something awful happening to her made him shudder. She was so bright, so earnest, so full of life. He found himself thinking about what he had been like at her age and he was struck by the contrast between them. She seemed so much more knowledgeable, so much more sophisticated. He smiled at this thought. 'You know the first time I travelled on a train,' he told her, 'I was so excited I could not sit still.'

As he said this, the girl glanced round at the other passengers. She felt sure they were looking at her father. It seemed to her that his voice was much too loud for a conversation on a train and she was embarrassed by his heavy accent. Why did he have to show her up like this? She found herself wishing, as she often did, that her father could be like everyone else's.

She decided to go to the buffet car to get away from the situation and she stood up. But there was something about the look in his eyes that stopped her. He wanted so badly to share this experience. For the first time in her life she suddenly felt as if she was the parent and her father was the child. She sighed, but quietly so that he wouldn't hear her. She sat back down again. 'Tell me about it,' she said.

A couple of miles further along the line, a group of teenage boys was standing near the track. At their feet was a pile of scaffolding poles, planks of wood and bricks. One of them, a tall youth with cropped hair, whose lip seemed to curl upwards in a permanent sneer, made a hawking noise and spat on the ground. Then he trod the spittle into the earth with the sole of his shoe. He looked up. 'Decision time,' he announced.

He put out his index finger and waved it slowly from side to side, hesitating before each of the group in turn as they watched him in silence. Finally the finger came to rest, pointing at a thin boy with brown hair and very pale blue eyes, who had a faintly puzzled expression on his face, as if he were not sure what exactly he was doing there.

'OK, weirdo, this time the finger stops at you,' the tall boy announced. Several of the others laughed, but more out of relief than because they thought it was funny.

A flicker of anger passed over the face of the boy he was pointing at. 'My name's Jacob,' he replied.

The tall boy shrugged. 'Whatever,' he said. 'It's your turn anyway.'

Jacob knew what he was expected to do. He was supposed to build a barricade across the line. But he didn't want to. He wished he could go back to the moment before he had climbed the embankment fence, the moment when he had stood at the end of Adelaide Avenue and told himself that he had to go through with this. But it was too late now. He was here and they were all waiting to see what he would do. There was nothing else for it. He bent down and picked up one of the planks.

A ragged cheer arose from the rest of the group.

As Jacob straightened up, he saw a smile of triumph playing across the lips of the boy with the cropped hair. There was something about that smile that made him stop. The smile said that putting the plank on the line was only the beginning. There would be so much more to follow.

Jacob looked away towards the wire fence he had climbed only a little earlier. A blackbird was sitting on the top, its head on one side. It seemed to be looking directly at him out of one bright, beady eye. As he hesitated, with the plank held tightly to his chest, the bird opened its beak and burst into song, filling the air with liquid notes that were almost breathtakingly beautiful.

Jacob listened and a dim memory began to wake in the

deepest part of his mind; he had the strangest feeling that he had lived through all of this before, that he had taken even harder decisions than this. The bird stopped singing and the feeling was gone, like a dream that vanishes upon waking. But something must have remained because it seemed to Jacob that he saw things more clearly now, that he felt stronger, less bothered about what others might think of him. He didn't have to do anything he didn't want to, he realised. It was as simple as that. At this thought, a great surge of relief washed over him and he dropped the plank. Then he turned, ignoring the jeering cries of the others, and began to climb back up the embankment towards the life he had left behind on the other side of the fence.

THE END